Rehabilitating Juvenile Justice

REHABILITATING
JUVENILE JUSTICE

CHARLES H. SHIREMAN
and
FREDERIC G. REAMER

New York   COLUMBIA UNIVERSITY PRESS   *1986*

Library of Congress Cataloging-in-Publication Data
Shireman, Charles.
Rehabilitating juvenile justice.

Bibliography: p.
Includes index.
1. Juvenile justice, Administration of—United States.
2. Juvenile delinquency—United States.   3. Rehabilita-
tion of juvenile delinquents—United States.
I. Reamer, Frederic G., 1953–   . II. Title.
HV9104.S446 1986   364.3'6'0973   86-6788
ISBN 0-231-06328-8

Book design by Laiying Chong.

Columbia University Press
New York   Guildford, Surrey
Copyright © 1986 Columbia University Press
All rights reserved

Contents

Preface

I would there were no age between ten and three and twenty, or that
youth would sleep out the rest; for there is nothing in between but getting
wenches with child, wronging the ancientry, stealing, fighting.
(Shakespeare, *The Winter's Tale*)

One might wonder, with considerable justification, what yet another
essay on juvenile justice has to offer beyond the others that have been
penned over the decades. Our literature is filled with thoughtful tomes
concerned with the nature and extent of juvenile misbehavior. For decades, contemporary social scientists have reported on investigations of
the origins of juvenile delinquency and exposed the naiveté of the "child
savers" who framed the first juvenile justice system. Legal scholars
continue to document procedural flaws in the handling of juvenile offenders by the police, courts, and correctional programs. Practitioners
in the field have generated countless reports on the design and delivery
of social services for these youths, and located gaps in our knowledge of
the art of rehabilitation.

Still, it seems to us that fundamental questions regarding the relationship between juvenile offenders and the state remain. Our purpose here
is to reopen dialogue on central issues concerned with the mission,
function, and competing values so vital to the formulation of juvenile
justice policy and practice. We set out neither to arrogantly raze nearly
a century's worth of effort in this field, nor simply to describe, accept,
and defend the status quo. Rather, we offer a hard but fair look at
where we have been in juvenile justice, where we now stand, and in
what direction we need to head.

To do so, we have drawn on our years-long efforts to locate and review
relevant theoretical, empirical, and practice literature. But out observations are also informed greatly by our own considerable experience as
practitioners in the juvenile and criminal justice fields. We have talked

with youths, federal and local officials who design and fund programs, professionals who staff them, and the neighbors who have mixed feelings about them. We have witnessed the despair, frustration, and hostility one often finds in the juvenile justice field, along with those glorious—but all too rare—moments of triumph. We believe that what we have learned over the years from our combined work in neighborhoods, police stations, court rooms, government agencies, community-based programs, and correctional institutions is essential to and enriches the observations and claims we offer here.

As educators, we have a keen interest in locating and generating knowledge that can be used in practice. Although we appreciate the value of theory for its own sake, our primary concern is with the thoughtful application of theory and research, and with the lives that are touched and sometimes scarred by the phenomenon of juvenile crime. We too are concerned about public safety and justice, and want as much as anyone who reads this book to be able to walk the streets of our neighborhoods without the gnawing sense of dread that too many of us know. Our principal goal here is to provide a reasoned, disciplined statement on a complex problem about which we care deeply. Our nation's youths are not destined to misbehave, and there is much we can do to intercede in their behalf. Our instincts tell us that Shakespeare was unnecessarily pessimistic.

Our book begins with a discussion of the emergence of juvenile justice as a field, along with an overview of trends in juvenile crime over the years (chapter 1). Our purpose is to lay the groundwork for a critical review of developments in the field since its formal inception in the late nineteenth century. This we begin in chapter 2, where we assess challenges to the concept of rehabilitation as an ideal in juvenile justice, and proposals to alter the traditional mission of the juvenile court. These various proposals and the goals of juvenile justice are then considered in light of what is known about the social and psychological development of juveniles (chapter 3).

We turn our attention next to what is currently known about the effectiveness of a wide range of approaches to responding to juvenile crime at the time of encounter with police, juvenile court authorities, and correctional officials (chapter 4). We focus especially on the persistent debate concerning the doctrine that "nothing works," in an effort to separate fact and fiction.

Beginning with chapter 5 we review a variety of proposals designed to rehabilitate a juvenile justice field considered by many to be in dire need of repair. Here we examine issues ranging from due process and sentencing guidelines to the handling of status offenders. In chapter 6 we take stock of lessons we have learned from past efforts to introduce reforms. We pay particular attention to obstacles and unintended consequences that previous attempts to bring about change have encountered, ones that we would do well to avoid in the future.

We conclude our discussion with a series of observations about what problems we can reasonably expect the juvenile justice system to solve on its own, in light of broad social, economic, political, and psychological circumstances that contribute to juvenile crime (chapter 7). The arguments we offer are couched in discussion of the extent to which it is prudent to hold juvenile offenders responsible for their misbehavior.

We would like to acknowledge the assistance we have received from several institutions that have supported our work: School of Social Service Administration, University of Chicago; School of Social Work, Rhode Island College; and Research Council, University of Missouri-Columbia. Edwina Simmons deserves special thanks for her clerical support. Our most heartfelt appreciation is due our respective families, who not only encouraged this endeavor but helped us along the way to discover and remember the things that matter.

Rehabilitating Juvenile Justice

CHAPTER 1

THE NATURE OF
JUVENILE CRIME

This yeare, the 29 of Januarie [1537/8] was arreigned at Westminster
in the afternoone a boye of Mr. Culpepers, Gentleman of the Kings Privie
Chamber, which had stolne his maisters purse and £11 of money, with a
jewell of the Kinges which was in the same purse, and there condemned
to death; but the morrowe after when he was brought to the place of
execution, which was at the ende of the tylt yeard afore the Kinges Pallace
at Westminster, and that the hangman was takinge the ladder from the
gallowes, the Kinge sent his pardon for the sayde boye, and so he was
saved from death, to the great comforte of all the people there present
&c. . . . (Sanders 1970)

All of us have had occasion to bristle upon hearing a neighbor, relative, or news commentator describe in disturbing detail a crime that led
to serious personal harm. Few events in life can be likened to true
victimization by which what is deeply meaningful to us, be it person or
property, is in some way violated, leaving us with resentment and anger
at a crime that all too often has no known author. Our fantasies run
wild under such circumstances, with thoughts of retributive acts that we
would engage in if only we knew the perpetrator. Thus, the present
era's daily tales of burgled homes, assaulted pedestrians, gang warfare,
and other forms of harassment have given rise to what appears to be
unprecedented fear of individuals who commit crimes.

Though apprehension about crime is widespread, there is little consensus about how the justice system should respond to violations. On
the one hand, there are clarion calls for punishment that is swift, certain, and severe. What offenders need is what they deserve, it is said.
And what they deserve is a full measure of our collective wrath: lengthy
sentences in penitentiaries and "correctional" facilities that neither
coddle their residents nor afford them life's ordinary amenities. But at

the same time, many of us have been schooled sufficiently to know that a wide variety of factors explain why people break laws. We are aware that high rates of unemployment, the ravages of inflation and other economic maladies, child abuse, family instability, and sundry other persistent social problems have something to do with the nagging burden of crime. Thus, there is tension between our inclination to punish those who break the law and our conflicting tendency to explain away their misbehavior because of the harsh social and economic problems that are apparently beyond any one person's control.

Our ambivalence toward offenders seems especially pronounced in our dealings with juveniles. As with Mr. Culpepers' boy who stole his master's purse in Tudor England, initial ire often gives way to relief once it has been decided to withhold harsh punishment. Such youngsters, we assume, cannot possibly appreciate the complex difference between right and wrong conduct. Their indiscretions are not the product of calculated efforts to hurt people; rather, they are the unfortunate consequences of that special chemistry that results when immaturity combines with youthful impulse and impressionability. Or are they?

This is the principal question to explore. It is our impression that the long-standing tradition of treating juvenile offenders more leniently than adults is on the decline. As we will take care to show, there is ample evidence that since at least Anglo-Saxon times, Western cultures have tended to treat juvenile offenders more leniently than adults, though certainly there have been noteworthy fluctuations. What we are currently experiencing in the United States, however, is a perceptible shift in our view of the youthful offender. Increasingly, we tend to see the juvenile delinquent as a willful perpetrator rather than as an unwilling victim of seductive and baneful influences. This shift has its exceptions. Yet, the general trend toward holding juveniles more rather than less responsible for their offenses seems undeniable. As a consequence, contemporary juvenile justice is at a crossroad. The choice that faces us is profound. What is at stake is nothing less than a judgment about the nature of our children, their culpability, and the culpability of our society. Indirectly, also at stake is a judgment about ourselves: about the limits of our ability to shape lives once we have created them and about our own culpability for whatever mischief our offspring bring about.

We begin with the premise, then, that many of the enduring traditions of the American juvenile justice system that have led to differential treatment of youthful offenders are in the midst of serious and sustained challenge. However, as with all premises that are to be taken seriously, this one too needs to be backed up with more than prima facie assertion.

The Rise of Child Saving

It is widely believed that the American tradition of distinguishing juveniles from adults in the eyes of the law has its origins in the late nineteenth-century inauguration of the juvenile court in Cook County, Illinois. However, many of the beliefs and practices that have characterized American juvenile justice preceded the creation of the first juvenile court in the United States by over ten centuries. The modern-day distinction between those above and below an age of majority is rooted at least in the seventh-century Laws of King Ine during his rule over England south of the Thames. Consider, for instance, King Ine's proscription concerning stealing, which set the age of majority at 10: "If any one steal, so that his wife and his children know it not, let him pay LX. shillings as 'wite' [punishment]. But if he steal with the knowledge of all his household, let them all go into slavery. A boy of X. years may be privy to a theft . . ." (Sanders 1970). And the use of juvenile probation, considered by many to be a modern invention, can be found in the tenth-century rule of King Athelstane of England. W. H. Stuart Garnett thus observed in his 1911 treatise on children and the law:

The desire to discriminate between the treatment of adult criminals and of young offenders capable of reformation, is no product of twentieth century sentimentality. Athelstane, son of Eadward, the giant warrior who clove the rock of Dunbar and became the almost mythical hero of the English people, not only attempted the reformation of juvenile offenders, but enacted in the tenth century substantial portions of the Children Act. The probation of young offenders, the requirement of security from parents, even to the very age specified in the Children Act, were the work of Athelstane and his council. (Garnett 1911:137)

Indeed, even the most ardent proponents of the classical school of criminology, those who regarded human beings as rational, calculating creatures responsible for their acts, acknowledged that children were exempt from the demands of utilitarian principles and should not be held to the same moral standards as adults. Jeremy Bentham, in his eighteenth-century classic, *An Introduction to the Principles of Morals and Legislation,* describes "infancy" as a stage during which an individual is not to be regarded as capable of calculating actions even though "matters of such importance as pain and pleasure are at stake" (Bentham [1789] 1973). And John Stuart Mill, in his nineteenth-century essay *On Liberty,* provides a disclaimer to his oft-quoted assertion that "the sole end for which mankind are warranted, individually or collectively, in interfering with the liberty of action of any of their number, is self-protection" (Mill [1849] 1973). He adds,

> It is perhaps hardly necessary to say that this doctrine is meant to apply only to human beings in the maturity of their faculties. We are not speaking of children, or of young persons below the age which the law may fix as that of manhood or womanhood. Those who are still in a state to require being taken care of by others, must be protected against their own actions as well as against external injury. (Mill [1849] 1973:484)

While children have been distinguished from adults for centuries, the age at which children should legally be considered adults has fluctuated throughout history. As Bentham asked in 1789,

> By what means then is it to be ascertained whether a man's intellect is in that state [infancy] or no? For exhibiting the quantity of sensible heat in a human body we have a very tolerable sort of instrument, the thermometer; but for exhibiting the quantity of intelligence, we have no such instrument. It is evident, therefore, that the line which separates the quantity of intelligence which *is* sufficient for the purposes of self-government from that which is *not* sufficient, must be, in a great measure, arbitrary. Where the insufficiency is the result of want of age, the sufficient quantity of intelligence, be it what it may, does not accrue to all at the same period of their lives. It becomes therefore necessary for legislators to cut the gordian knot, and fix upon a particular period, at which and not before, truly or not, every person whatever shall be deemed, as far as depends upon age, to be in possession of this sufficient quantity. (Bentham [1789] 1973:237)

What does seem clear is that in the United States the age of responsibility generally has risen over time. When Illinois was admitted to the Union in 1817, a child under 7 years was not considered responsible for his behavior. In 1827, a revision of the state code raised the age of criminal responsibility to 10 and, in 1831, children under 18 were excluded by statute from the state penitentiary (Platt 1977). The tendency to raise the age of majority has generally been consistent with the philosophical changes that accompanied the period of the enlightenment and its emphasis on human progress and individualism rather than inherent depravity and preordained destiny.

It is apparent, then, that the nineteenth-century development of the juvenile court did not signify for the first time a fundamental change in the *view* of children and their responsibility for their misbehavior. Instead, historical accounts of the origin of the juvenile court indicate that its development represented a change in methods of *handling* troublesome youths.

Though there is considerable debate concerning whether those who contributed to the development of the first juvenile court can defend their claims that the court embodied a set of innovations that markedly changed for the better the ways in which juveniles were treated (Platt 1977; Fox 1974), it is clear that, for better or worse, there was an inordinately high level of agreement at the time that children ought to be "saved" and not punished for their misdeeds. They were to be helped and loved and gently removed from the pernicious effects of squalid conditions. For example, at the Second International Penitentiary Congress held in Stockholm in 1878, it was "resolved that delinquent children should not be punished but educated so as to enable them to 'gain an honest livelihood and to become of use to society instead of an injury to it' " (Platt 1977:50). Even for those youths removed from their homes it was noted by the Board of Public Charities of the state of Illinois in 1879 that "the object of reformatory institutions is well stated; it is not punishment for past offenses, but training for future usefulness" (Platt 1977:106). And in 1898, a delegate to the National Prison Association urged that we should "point out to the children . . . all that is beautiful in nature and art. . . . Teach them to love mother and the home, and to hope for heaven. . . . Give the little fellows good companionship, decent, comfortable quarters, clean beds and wholesome food. Smile on them, speak to them, and let sunshine into their souls" (Platt 1977:70).

This pervasive climate of opinion persisted. Soon after the first juvenile court began operation in Cook County, its first chief probation officer, Timothy Hurley, considered that

> Those interested in saving the little ones from the fearful future which seemed to be yawning for them realized that the fountain head of the evil, vice and crime as well as of virtue and honor, was to be found in the home surroundings of the child. The wisest efforts to reform abuses were thwarted by homes that were depraved. It was realized that the real criminal was not the individual himself, but the entire social body that permitted conditions to exist which could produce only criminals. (Hurley 1907:57)

It is also evident that at least the first two judges of the Cook County juvenile court agreed that the legal proceedings were to be nothing worse than benign. Richard Tuthill, the first judge of the court, described the manner in which he heard a youth's case:

> I first speak to him in a kindly and considerate way, endeavoring to make him feel that there is no purpose on the part of anyone about him to punish, but rather to benefit and help, to make him realize that the State—that is, the good people of the State—are interested in him, and want to do only what will be of help to him now and during his entire life. (Tuthill 1904:1)

Julian Mack, the second juvenile court judge in Cook County, did not depart from this approach:

> In a word, as was well said in the course of the debates on the Children's Bill in the House of Commons: We want to say to the child that if the world or the world's law has not been his friend in the past, it shall be now. We say that it is the duty of this Parliament and that this Parliament is determined to lift, if possible and rescue him, to shut the prison door, and to open the door of hope. (Mack 1909:104)

It seems clear that these characterizations of the youthful offender as one who should incur society's aid instead of its wrath were not exceptional ones voiced only by those working closely with the youths.

Rather, as Hurley indicated in his 1907 review of the Illinois Juvenile Court Law, the sentiment was widespread:

In this movement, destined to contribute largely to the fame and glory of Chicago and Cook County, there was no politics and no dissension. If rivalry there was, either between the bodies which sent delegates to the joint committee or between the members of the joint committee as individuals, it was the laudable rivalry of how best to advance the humane enterprise which was dear to the heart of each and everyone of those interested. It was peculiarly a Chicago spirit—the spirit which Chicago knows how well to put forth where interests which she holds sacred are concerned.

Time or change will not weaken this spirit: they can only strengthen it. Though the personnel representing public sentiment in elective and appointive offices must necessarily be different at different times, the sentiment itself when grounded upon right and justice and charity, remains ever the same. The humane feelings back of the Juvenile Court law and of the movement generally to do justice by erring young in their first wanderings from the straight and narrow path is stronger in Chicago today than it ever was. Recent political changes have transferred its destinies not to strangers but to friends who have already given proof of their devotion to the interests of the child. (Hurley 1907:51–52)

This high degree of consensus was also evident in the proceedings of both the Chicago Bar Association and the Illinois State Legislature. The Illinois State Senate passed the famed "Act to Regulate the Treatment and Control of Dependent, Neglected, and Delinquent Children," resulting in the creation of the first juvenile court, without much delay and by a vote of 32–1. Subsequently the House passed the bill 121–0 on April 14, 1899. The special committee on juvenile courts of the Chicago Bar Association submitted a report at the association's twenty-sixth annual meeting the following October, stating that "The whole trend and spirit of the act is that the state, acting through the Juvenile Court, exercises that tender solicitude and care over its neglected, dependent and delinquent wards that a wise and loving parent would exercise with reference to his own children under similar circumstances" (Hurley 1907:47).

The perceptions of the young offender as a child not culpable for his acts and as a victim of unintended but miasmic social conditions did not change dramatically during the first half-century of the juvenile court's life. The mission of the court promulgated in 1899 was staunchly defended: criticisms primarily addressed the need for improved methods of court administration. That this was the prevailing mood is apparent when one examines two journals that devoted issues to the fiftieth anniversary of the court. The contents of the "Special Issue Commemorating the Fiftieth Anniversary of the Juvenile Court" of *Federal Probation,* published in 1949, were entirely in the spirit of the late nineteenth-century proponents of the court. No mention is made of increasing the child's responsibility in the articles prepared by Charles Chute of the National Probation and Parole Association ("The Juvenile Court in Retrospect"), Katharine Lenroot, the Chief of the Children's Bureau ("The Juvenile Court Today"), William Healey, Director Emeritus of the Judge Baker Guidance Clinic ("Thoughts About Juvenile Courts"), Gustav Schramm, who was both the Juvenile Court Judge of Allegheny County (Pittsburgh) and the President of the National Council of Juvenile Court Judges ("The Juvenile Court Idea"), or Harrison Allen Dobbs of Louisiana State University ("In Defense of Juvenile Courts"). In the same year, the *Annals of the American Academy of Political Science* devoted an issue to juvenile delinquency and the juvenile court to "signalize the fiftieth anniversary of the most important judicial agency for dealing with delinquents that has grown out of American experience," and lent the court another vote of confidence.

Four years later, in 1953, there appeared Alfred Kahn's study of the juvenile court in New York City, *A Court for Children.* In it the mission of the court continues to be uncritically accepted:

> As for the underlying concept of delinquency and of how individuals can be helpful, the statement of Miriam Van Waters more than a quarter of a century ago represents this study's viewpoint: "That human conduct is caused; that ordering and forbidding cannot change it; that in order to modify behavior one must understand it and deal *gently* and comprehendingly with the human beings who experience it." (emphasis added; Kahn 1953:14)

It is also worth noting that the vast majority of the academic literature on delinquency and its causes published during the period between 1899 and the 1950s lent support to the view that the juvenile delinquent is not responsible for his behavior and is somehow compelled to act by forces beyond his control. In the early twentieth century the works of the Italian positivists—Cesare Lombroso, Enrico Ferri, Raffaele Garofalo—foreshadowed a series of writings that characterized delinquency as the product of physiological, psychological, and environmental forces (Quinney 1970). The so-called Chicago school of the 1920s, including Ernest Burgess, Clifford Shaw, and Henry McKay, emphasized ecological factors that were thought to account for delinquency rates, and the famous statement issued by Robert Merton in 1938 concerning social structure and anomie stressed the problems arising from a lack of correspondence between goals inculcated in individuals by the societies in which they are reared and the means by which those goals can be reached (Sutherland and Cressey 1966). The late 1940s and early 1950s produced a burgeoning of theoretical explanations by psychoanalysts asserting a connection between poor character formation and delinquent behavior (Berman 1959). Also during this time, William Sheldon (1949) introduced his hypothesis concerning the link between somatotypes—the endomorph, ectomorph, and mesomorph—and varieties of delinquent behavior. Toward the end of the 1950s the delinquency literature contained prominent claims about the lack of sufficient roles to facilitate the passage of adolescents into adult status (Bloch and Niederhoffer 1958), and the problems endemic to female-dominated households (Parsons 1949). In 1955, Albert Cohen published his *Delinquent Boys,* in which he sought to explain the lower-class boy's delinquent behavior as a reaction formation against middle-class values, and the analysis of opportunity structure was elaborated upon by Richard Cloward and Lloyd Ohlin in their 1960 *Delinquency and Opportunity.*

As one reviews these major theoretical formulations it becomes apparent that the view of the delinquent as a willful, calculating actor is conspicuously absent. These formulations generally reinforce the image of the youthful offender first espoused by the "child savers." Whatever criticisms were leveled against the juvenile court tended not to pertain to the court's assumption that children were, in effect, to be saved, but instead to more "practical" problems concerning the scope of the juvenile court's jurisdiction, due process, and the court's ability to provide quality services delivered by qualified personnel (Rosenheim 1962).

The Decline of Child Saving

In the mid-1960s, a gradual but perceptible shift in attitude toward the juvenile began. In May 1965, the Gallup poll reported that for the first time "crime" (which, we assume, included delinquency in the minds of most respondents) was listed as the nation's most important problem (Wilson 1975). This fact is not only significant in itself; it also apparently marks a lowering of the nation's threshold of tolerance. Citizens were becoming less willing to treat kindly "the poor child who has been through so much." And when we consider that the proportion of crimes committed by those under age 21 increased dramatically during the decade of the 1960s (Wellford 1973), it is possible that the prevailing tendency was to imagine that those who were committing the crimes so productive of fear and anger were, more than ever before, juveniles. With the combination of the increase in crime rates in general, the increase in the proportion of offenses committed by juveniles, and the concomitant increase in public concern, the average citizen apparently began to resent the juvenile offender more deeply. It became difficult to consider the youthful offender as a child in need only of love, kindness, and the spirit of child saving. These youths were all too often committing frightening and visible offenses that were, literally and figuratively, hitting closer and closer to home.

The latter part of the 1960s seems to have been marked by three admissions essentially new to this nation's view of the juvenile offender. They were preceded by one admission that was not new, one that had, in fact, been heard since the opening of the first House of Refuge in New York in 1825 and of the Lyman Reform School in Massachusetts in 1847: that despite official rhetoric to the contrary, youths in the state correctional institutions were often not receiving the treatment that a wise and loving parent would exercise with reference to his own children. Youths were being punished, and the thin veneer provided by euphemistic titles for staff and institutions could not camouflage what was taking place. Thus, in 1964, Francis Allen eloquently pointed out in his *Borderland of Criminal Justice* that

> Whatever one's motivation, however elevated one's objectives, if the measures taken result in the compulsory loss of the child's

liberty, the involuntary separation of a child from his family or even the supervision of a child's activities by a probation worker, the impact on the affected individual is essentially a punitive one. Good intentions and a flexible vocabulary do not alter this reality. This is particularly so when as is often the case, the institution to which the child is committed is, in fact, a peno-custodial establishment. We shall escape much confusion here if we are willing to give candid recognition to the fact that the business of the juvenile court inevitably consists, to a considerable degree, in dispensing punishment. (Allen 1964:18)

On the heels of this first admission appeared one that many professionals frankly knew how to do little but punish, that in fact they lacked the full knowledge required to rehabilitate juvenile offenders without coercion. Considering this, concluded the President's Commission on Law Enforcement and Administration of Justice (1967), the community at least had to protect itself:

In theory the court's operations could justifiably be informal, its findings and decisions made without observing ordinary procedural safeguards, because it would act only in the best interest of the child. In fact, it frequently does nothing more nor less than deprive a child of liberty without due process of law—knowing not what else to do and needing, whether admittedly or not, to act in the community's interest even more imperatively than the child's. ... The limitations, both in theory and in execution, of strictly rehabilitative treatment methods, combined with public anxiety over the seemingly irresistible rise in juvenile criminality, have produced a rupture between the theory and the practice of juvenile court dispositions. While statutes, judges, and commentators still talk the language of compassion, help, and treatment, it has become clear that in fact the same purposes that characterize the use of the criminal law for adult offenders—retribution, condemnation, deterrence, incapacitation—are involved in the disposition of juvenile offenders too. These are society's ultimate techniques for protection against threatening conduct; it is inevitable that they should be used against threats from the young as well as the old when other resources appear unavailing. (President's Commission 1967:8–9)

The next admission included statements maintaining that the community should not only, by default, protect itself, since efforts to save children appeared to be ineffective, but that it was indeed acceptable to give *priority* to protection of the community, whether or not attempts at benign treatment were effective. This is a significant turning point; the community began claiming a *right* to protection that superseded its duty to "save" youth. As the President's Commission put it,

The juvenile court is a court of law, charged like other agencies of criminal justice with protecting the community against threatening conduct. Rehabilitating offenders through individualized handling is one way of providing protection, and appropriately the primary way in dealing with children. But the guiding consideration for a court of law that deals with threatening conduct is nonetheless protection of the community. The juvenile court, like other courts, is therefore obliged to employ all the means at hand, not excluding incapacitation, for achieving that protection. What should distinguish the juvenile from the criminal courts is greater emphasis on rehabilitation, not exclusive preoccupation with it. (1967:9)

The final admission in the late 1960s even went beyond claiming that the community had a fundamental right, above all else, to protect itself. It included statements asserting that the community should also condemn and punish the behavior of certain of its troublesome youths. Thus, after recommending that the court's jurisdiction over the behavior of juveniles be narrowed, the President's Commission stated:

The cases that fall within the narrowed jurisdiction of the court and filter through the screen of informal, prejudicial, informal disposition methods would largely involve offenders for whom more vigorous measures seem necessary. Court adjudication and disposition of those offenders should no longer be viewed solely as a diagnosis and prescription for cure, but should be frankly recognized as an authoritative court judgment expressing society's claim to protection. While rehabilitative efforts should be vigorously pursued in deference to the youth of the offenders and in keeping with a general commitment to individualized treatment of all offenders, the incapacitative, deterrent, and *condemnatory* aspects of the judgment should not be disguised. (emphasis added; 1967:2)

This revealing conclusion was followed by an article in the same volume by Robert Vinter (1967) in which he commented on community support for the punishment of juvenile offenders:

> Considerable evidence indicates widespread public expectations that juvenile courts should give special emphasis to maintenance of public order. This concern receives very strong local support, and attempts to balance it against other aims often evoke indignant community protest. Further, some among the general citizenry appear to have definite and ready-made notions of how public order can best be maintained: by prompt and strenuous action, by "setting examples," by strict application of *punishments,* and so forth. (emphasis added) (Vinter 1967:85)

The publication of this report signaled a proliferation of programs and procedures that have radically altered the complexion of juvenile justice in the United States. In response to the decline in faith that the juvenile court and correctional institutions were capable of treating youthful offenders humanely, efficaciously, and with proper regard for public safety and for the youths' legal rights before the bar, a series of goals emerged that have served since then to shape the juvenile justice landscape: decriminalization, diversion, due process, and deinstitutionalization.

Decriminalization entails the removal of certain behaviors from the list of offenses for which youths can be found to be delinquent or to be "minors in need of supervision" (status offenders). The argument has been that acts such as running away from home, truancy, and ungovernability either are without victims or are problems that would best be dealt with by private or public social service agencies rather than the juvenile justice system, and therefore should not be classified as offenses. Proponents of decriminalization have claimed that reclassification would have two major benefits: (1) the volume of cases that currently strain many juvenile courts, probation departments, and correctional facilities would be substantially reduced, allowing more time for the handling of more serious cases; and (2) providing services to youths under the auspices of social service agencies rather than the juvenile court would help to diminish the chances that youths will be adversely affected by the stigmatizing labels and maleficent experiences frequently thought to be associated with being processed by formal juvenile justice agencies.

Diversion includes any attempt to steer youths away from formal handling by the police or the juvenile court. Youths are generally referred to diversion programs—which may be operated by public or private agencies and provide services such as crisis counseling, family counseling, vocational training, tutoring, dispute mediation, or supervision of restitution—at the time of encounter with police or by intake personnel at the juvenile court. Youths may be referred to police or court diversion programs with no strings attached (known as true diversion), or they may be referred with the stipulation that their case may be reinstated if the expectations of program personnel are not met (pseudo diversion). Once again, the principal rationale is to reduce the caseloads of juvenile courts and correctional facilities, and avoid as much as possible the stigma associated with being labeled a troublesome youth.

The goal of *due process* emerged because of widespread concern that juvenile offenders were not being afforded legal protections or procedural safeguards that were routinely available to adults, though, despite rhetoric to the contrary, youths were being subjected to the same sorts of judicial penalties imposed upon adult offenders (for example, pretrial detention, fines and restitution orders, and incarceration in correctional facilities). Several Supreme Court decisions rendered in the 1960s were seminal, in that they inspired overhauls in many juvenile courts throughout the nation, especially in relation to procedures for waiving juveniles to adult criminal courts (*Kent v. United States*, 1966); juveniles' right to a timely and precise notice of charges, counsel, protection against self-incrimination, and confrontation and cross-examination of witnesses (*In Re Gault*, 1967); and the requirement of "proof beyond a reasonable doubt" in delinquency hearings, rather than a mere preponderance of evidence (*In Re Winship*, 1970). Thus, the widespread endorsement of the doctrine of *parens patriae* (the state acting as benevolent parent) that characterized the birth of the juvenile court and the first half-century of its life gave way rather suddenly in the mid-1960s, as indicated by a series of decisions that have served to introduce considerable formality into juvenile court hearings and a strong hint of the adversarial proceedings of adult criminal trials.

The fourth goal, *deinstitutionalization*, rounded out the ideological agenda set in the 1960s. This principle was tied closely to the goal of diversion, in that it sought to remove as many juveniles as possible from what was considered to be the malevolent grasp of the formal juvenile justice system and, more specifically, the clutches of correctional facilities. Despite euphemisms such as "training school," "youth development center," and "boys' home," those who were in close touch with the daily workings of these institutions knew how little good many or even most of them fostered, in spite of the frequently commendable intentions of their staffs. Candid recognition of the fact that little was being "corrected" within these facilities and that the goals of custody, discipline, and punishment typically overshadowed whatever fantasies staff had about rehabilitation led to substantial efforts to avoid sending adjudicated offenders to institutions in the first place and to develop alternatives for those who were currently residents. As a result of these efforts, fueled largely by provisions of the 1974 Juvenile Justice and Delinquency Prevention Act and its amendments, both residential and nonresidential programs have developed nationwide as alternatives to institutionalization. These have included day probation, vocational and educational upgrading, wilderness programs, group and shelter homes for specific populations (for example, runaways, drug or alcohol abusers, "serious" offenders, severely disturbed offenders), case management, and restitution programs.

Though our forthcoming discussion will make it clear that serious questions can be raised about the success of the various attempts that have been made to meet the goals of decriminalization, diversion, due process, and deinstitutionalization, it is apparent that the pursuit of these goals has done much to alter the way in which juvenile offenders are treated in the United States. Many jurisdictions have successfully removed certain offenses from the purview of the juvenile justice system (principally status offenses), developed police and court diversion programs, increased procedural safeguards, and designed and implemented a variety of alternatives to institutionalization. Yet, the current mood is generally far less sympathetic to the unbridled pursuit of these goals. In fact, present treatment of juvenile offenders is marked by considerable ambivalence. Many contemporary practitioners have retained some of the deep-seated beliefs of the nineteenth-century "child savers," in particular the belief that in meaningful ways juveniles do differ from adults and thus require different handling by the justice system. The child may truly have diminished capacity to calculate the future costs to others or to himself of his own actions. His behavior may more frequently and more evidently result in very real part from peer pressure, the shortcomings of parents, and other environmental (for example, economic) circumstances. Formal court processing to determine whether or not the child actually committed the offense of which he is accused may be a necessary but very partial response to a situation that severely limited his capacity to opt for a conforming style of life. Thus, a "just deserts" model for the juvenile justice system may overlook long histories of injustice that contributed to a youth's problem behavior. In line with this view, the spirit that led in the first place to development of the juvenile justice system persists to a considerable degree. Moreover, the fervor that surrounded the efforts begun in the 1960s to establish diversion and other community-based programs for all but the relatively few offenders who represent a genuine and severe threat to the community remains prevalent.

At the same time, however, substantial efforts are under way to reverse this trend. In a number of states, legislatures have adopted or are contemplating "get tough" policies designed to respond with severity and certainty to the scourge of juvenile delinquency. They have, for example, introduced mandatory sentences for the commission of serious offenses and for chronic offenders, and the lowered age of majority and standards for waiving youths to criminal courts for trial as adults. As a consequence, contemporary juvenile justice seems framed by a paradox, characterized by a series of forceful movements in large part consistent with the beliefs of the nineteenth-century era of the child savers and the reforms of the 1960s and 1970s. However, we are at the same time more inclined now than at any other time in this century to call for "adult punishment for adult crimes," even if the perpetrator is below the legal age of majority. What is also significant about the current ambivalence is that it is not manifest simply in the opposition of factions that hold different beliefs about the treatment of juvenile offenders; it is also to be found *within* many of us who, for professional or personal reasons, concern ourselves with the problem of juvenile delinquency. This striking ambivalence seems to be the Scylla and Charybdis of contemporary juvenile justice, pulling us first this way and then that, catching us between our inclination to seek rational explanations along with benign, compassionate panaceas, and our temptation to simply repudiate youthful nuisances.

Certainly the manner in which we choose to resolve our ambivalence toward juvenile offenders has serious implications for the policies and programs we develop in response to their misdeeds. However, our ambivalence cannot be resolved simply by reflecting on our emotion-laden vision of children and their culpability for illegal activities; in addition, we must examine closely the assumptions we make about the actual volume of juvenile crime over time, the characteristics of the youths who engage in delinquent acts, and the nature of offenses committed.

The Scope of the Problem

For at least the past two decades, juvenile delinquency and youth crime have been major sources of public alarm. "Young toughs" are envisioned as rendering the citizen fearful of riding subways, strolling in city parks, walking the streets after dark, or even, in many parts of the city, resting at ease in one's home at night. *Time* magazine (1977) writes of "The Youth Crime Plague," and the *Boston Globe*'s description of "a generation of street corner teenagers who have seized control of the sidewalks and parks after dark, converting them to their own use" (quoted in Liazos 1979:337) remains contemporary as we move toward the mid-1980s.

None of this is wholly new. It is probably in the nature of things that the elders of most societies should fear the young. Youths are certain to displace them. Further, the youth's struggle to form his own emerging adult self-image is quite likely to demand aggressive rejection of control by his elders. Resultant intergenerational tensions are heightened in periods such as the present, which are characterized by extremes of anxiety about crime in general. Since the mid-1960s, Gallup, Harris, and other polling organizations have consistently reported the "crime problem" as among the most prominent concerns of the American people. Fear of crime and the criminal are among the elements most corrosive of the American way of life. Thus, for example, in sampling surveys almost 30 percent of the respondents of small towns report being afraid to walk about in nearby neighborhoods at night. In large cities, the figure exceeds 60 percent; among the urban elderly it is almost 75 percent (Skogon and Maxfield 1981:47). The "Figgie Report on Fear of Crime" summarized a sampling survey of 1,047 randomly selected American households. The survey found that "there is clearly a deep-seated fear of crime in America, a fear that is growing and is slowly paralyzing every level of society" (Research and Forecasts, Inc. 1983:11). Fifty-two percent of the residents of the sample households owned guns for self-protection and 40 percent said they were highly fearful that they would become victims of violent crimes of murder, rape, robbery, and assault, and that, as a result, they felt unsafe in their everyday environment.

There is much harsh reality behind current anxieties about crime in general and youth crime in particular. It is impossible to evade the fact that our society has somehow managed to produce a disturbing number of dreadfully hurtful young people. It is also impossible to evade the intensity of the societal reaction crime engenders—the often fierce determination that *something* must be done about a problem that is bad enough in objective reality and that often seems heightened in its subjective assessment. Thus, for example, in recent years, traffic fatalities have ranged from approximately 44,000 to 54,000 a year (*Wall Street Journal* 1982:1). By rough comparison, in 1979, of the some 21,400 murder victims in the United States, about 12.5 percent, or some 2,700 represented "murder by a stranger" (FBI 1979:7, 11). Comparisons of non-fatal injuries or property losses from crime and from auto crashes would probably produce somewhat similar proportions. Compared to traffic injury or loss—or, for that matter, to accidents within the home—serious injury or loss from crime is somewhat rare, even in today's turbulent times. But the societal fear, anger, and frustration resulting from "predatory crime" is vastly greater than that aroused by traffic accidents or other common threats to our persons or property. There is something about the offender, either juvenile or adult, that arouses fear and hatred. We may recognize in him the threat to the ties that bind society together. His unrestrained behavior may force awareness of the thinness of the veneer of control that prevents our own and others' reversion to savage, unrestrained impulse gratification.

Social policy with regard to the offender, then, must often be formed in a climate of suspicion, fear, and frustrated anger. Too often, reason and calculation come in a poor second to deep feelings. Ends pursued are largely latent rather than acknowledged. Sharply conflicting, often only distantly rational expectations are placed upon the agents of the justice system, who are variously beset with demands that they simply punish the offender, that they protect society by incapacitating him, that they "make an example" of him so that others will be deterred from offending, that they "rehabilitate" him—or that they find some way of preventing misbehavior before it occurs. Frustratingly, however, delinquency and youth crime appear to fluctuate with embarrassingly little regard for any measures taken by law enforcement or juvenile or criminal justice.

As with any other widespread social pathology, a rational approach to the development of social policy with regard to youth crime would seem to require, as an initial step, analysis of the various manifestations of the problem, of trends in its incidence and distribution, and of its causes. The policy analyst first turning to this set of questions may be rewarded with an enormous volume of data, repeatedly and intricately analyzed by conscientious scholars who have devoted much of their professional lives to the task. Unfortunately, however, initial gratification at this discovery will, upon closer acquaintance, yield to a more pessimistic realization that much of what is "generally known" about delinquency is simply not so, that major lacunae exist in the data necessary to assess it, and that such data as are available are subject to conflicting interpretations.

The successful development of an index that will depict with reasonable accuracy the distribution of and trends in delinquency and crime has been a mirage that has flickered tantalizingly before the eyes of scholars for several generations. In important respects, the goal may be unattainable. The rubrics "delinquency" and "crime" refer to enormous ranges of human behaviors. Such behaviors are variously perceived and defined by differing societies at differing times and in differing places. They include "robberies" ranging from the aggressive appropriation of the schoolboy's lunch money by his peer, to the strong-arming of the senior citizen on the public street, to the armed stickup. They include the acts of the exhibitionist, the "voyeur," and the assaultive rapist. The spontaneous adolescent "borrowing" of a car for "joy-riding" and the auto theft for the chop-shop must be counted, as must the killing by an insanely jealous spouse and that by the gangland enforcer. With all these must be lumped the income tax evader, the check-kiter, and the conspirator in restraint of trade. This melange of behaviors has few common elements enabling their combination into a single meaningful scale.

The problem becomes more confusing if one includes in the total—as in the United States many but not all states do—such juvenile status offenses as being "ungovernable" by one's parents, running away from home, or truanting from school. Even greater complications ensue if one essays comparisons with distant places or distant times and discovers that among recognized "crimes" may fall blasphemy, entering the mosque with shod feet, expressing—or even harboring—negative thoughts about the sovereign, or "clipping" gold coins.

Nonetheless, attempts to discern the tangible behind the shadowy reality persist. Data are produced. They are sometimes sources of illusion, but if their speculative and shifting foundations are kept in mind they do provide some basis for the complicated and tentative judgments necessary to at least beginning understanding.

In the United States, the most frequently quoted data come from the Uniform Crime Reports (UCR), published annually by the Federal Bureau of Investigation. The UCRs are aggregations of data provided voluntarily to the FBI by several thousand law enforcement agencies representing the greater part of the population of the United States. They make available two basic sorts of information: that upon selected serious crimes reported to the police as having been committed and that upon persons arrested.

Citations of trends in crimes committed are commonly derived from the UCRs index, constructed from reports upon the numbers of serious crimes in eight categories that police learn have been committed in a given year. Included are the violent crimes of murder, forcible rape, robbery, and aggravated assault, and the property crimes of burglary, larceny-theft, motor vehicle theft, and (since 1979) arson. These are termed the "index crimes," and are thought to provide at least a crude measure of trends in serious crime generally. They may do so, and the UCRs are the source of many reports in the press upon crime rates, at least until recently always reported to be zooming upward. The validity and therefore the utility of these data are severely limited, however, by the unknown relationship between the number of crimes actually committed, the number of those reported to the police, and the number of those so reported actually recorded and reported *by* the police. Recent surveys during which samples of the U.S. population are asked to enumerate incidents of their having been criminally victimized seem to show that only about half of all serious crimes are reported to police, the proportion varying widely by type of crime. And of the crimes that are reported to the police, slightly less than 20 percent result in the identification and arrest of an accused perpetrator. Obviously, no one knows from the UCRs what the actual volume or rate of crime in the country is, and obviously we know even less about who commits most crimes. As Josiah Stamp noted in Britain years ago with his tongue only partly in his cheek: "The government are very keen on amassing statistics. They collect, raise them to the nth power, take the cube root and prepare wonderful diagrams. But you must never forget that every one of these figures comes in the first instance from the village watchman, who just puts down what he damn pleases" (Chaiken and Chaiken 1983).

While the UCRs, then, provide only the crudest information about the volume, distribution, or trends in crime, they do in their arrest reports make available at least a blurred profile of persons whose activities lead to their arrest and their being drawn into the toils of the justice system. Their numbers are considerable. Thus, in 1984, for example, enforcement agencies reported an estimated 11.6 million arrests for alleged criminal violations other than traffic offenses—49.5 arrests for every 1,000 inhabitants of our country (FBI 1984:161).

It does appear that children and youths account for a distressing proportion of all arrests. In 1984, for example, juveniles under the age of 18 may be estimated to have constituted some 29.7 percent and those 15, 16, and 17 to have made up 4.6 percent of the U.S. population (Spencer 1984:41). Those under 18 account for 31.0 percent of that year's estimated 2,359,500 arrests for index crimes, and those 15, 16, and 17 for 18.0 percent of such arrests (FBI 1984:161). Figures based on population projections (Spencer 1984) and arrest rates (FBI 1984) show that 31.9 percent of all index property-crime arrests were of juveniles under 18, and 18.1 percent of such arrests were made among the 4.6 percent of the population ages 15, 16, and 17. The latter group also accounted for some 11.3 percent of the year's violent crime arrests (FBI 1984:172).

It is true, of course, that juvenile arrest statistics may create a less satisfactory index of juvenile crime than do arrest statistics for adults. Juveniles' misdeeds may be somewhat more likely to be detected than those of adults. More important, juveniles tend to commit their offenses in pairs or groups, just as they play their games and spend their lives. One offense may lead to the arrest of two, three, or more juveniles, and thus to the inflation of juveniles' apparent contribution to official statistics (Zimring 1981:867–73). But for all these caveats, the data do at least constitute evidence that juveniles in the United States resemble our adults in that an unfortunate number of them engage in unlawful behaviors making them the subjects of the law enforcement and justice system.

The probable commission of a considerable proportion of the country's crime by juveniles seems to be further evidenced by National Crime Survey data. These data are derived from interviews carried out by the Census Bureau for the Department of Justice. Every six months, the residents of a stratified national sample of 60,000 households are asked to report instances of their having been victimized by personal or household crimes. As with the FBI Crime Index data, the perpetrators of most victim-reported crimes are unknown. However, the victim surveys furnish some data on selected crimes in which there is contact between the victim and the offender. For these personal contact crimes, victims are asked to estimate the age of their aggressors. In 1981, people estimated as under 18 years of age accounted for some 16 percent of all single-offender crimes of violence (rape, robbery, and assault).

While juveniles may contribute somewhat disproportionately to the total of arrests and to some victim-reported crimes, their contribution to very serious crime in the United States may be a lesser proportion than the above statistics suggest. From UCR index arrest data, the crimes for which juveniles aged 11–17 appear "overrepresented" are motor theft, which includes temporary theft for "joy-riding"; larceny-theft, which includes a considerable portion of quite petty thefts; burglary, which is a serious crime but may include such incidents as the entering of an abandoned warehouse by a group of boys, almost as a lark; and one violent crime: robbery (Smith et al. 1979:93). This last crime is generally one of the most serious, but may include, for juveniles, incidents at the less serious end of the scale for that offense class (such as unarmed but forceful appropriation by the schoolboy of another's lunch money). National Crime Surveys (victim surveys) also show that "juvenile crime is less serious in terms of weapons use, thefts, financial losses, and injuries than is adult crime" (American Correctional Association 1981:11).

Some further insight into the prevalence of law-violation among juveniles is available through the considerable number of self-report studies undertaken in the United States during the past twenty-five years or so. In these, scheduled interviews or questionnaires have been administered to various local or, in two instances, national samples of American juveniles, usually those enrolled in school. Youngsters are asked to report, confidentially, the numbers and types of delinquent acts they have "ever" engaged in, or have engaged in during a specified period in the past. The data thus obtained must be employed circumspectly, of course. It may be that young people vary in the completeness with which they report their behavior; the questionnaire and interview guides sometimes differ considerably from study to study, many placing considerable emphasis on minor offenses; and study populations vary widely.

Nonetheless, the self-report studies do yield at least some significant data. Not surprisingly, almost all the studies show that law-breaking is much more widespread than is shown by official statistics such as those based upon arrests. It appears that nine out of ten illegal acts by juveniles which could be chargeable in court go undetected by police (Empey 1978:159). Official records obviously show only a small fraction of the total volume of juvenile law-violative behavior. Any increase in police surveillance of juveniles, or any other change in circumstances leading to an increase in the size of that fraction, could result in an apparent "juvenile crime wave," quite without any change in actual juvenile behavior.

It is also apparent from the self-report studies that some degree of law-violative behavior is a part of the growing-up years of most American youths. One cannot accurately conceive of two sharply delineated groups of young people: the delinquents and the nondelinquents. Nor does an "everybody's doing it" attitude usefully reflect reality. More accurately, one might think of a continuum, at one end of which are the majority of youths who have been involved in at least some law-violative behavior, usually nonserious in nature. Further along the continuum would be those more frequently and more seriously delinquent, and at the extreme are the few constituting a chronic threat to the property and/or persons of their fellow citizens.

It is probable, however, that these data on the broad bounds of the problem become more significant when supplemented by those available on trends over time in the development of the problem and those upon its distribution among population subgroups.

Trends in Delinquency Rates

In 1981, the President of the United States pronounced crime to be an "American epidemic" and an Attorney General's Task Force on Violent Crime spoke of "the wave of serious, violent crime we are now experiencing . . . ," reporting that "The public is well aware that crime has reached alarming proportions in American society" (Galvin and Polk 1982:160, 137). There is widespread belief that the problem of crime is of such explosive dimensions as to be almost unique to our time and our country.

Data published by the FBI show some basis for the belief in burgeoning crime rates. The crime rate per 100,000 persons in the population was estimated to be 1,887.2 for 1960; by 1975 it had rocketed to 5,281.0 (FBI 1975:49). However, the task of assessing changes in rates of crime and delinquency is enormously complicated by the difficulty in selecting a proper time perspective from which to view the problem. Somewhat astonishingly to consumers of many annual UCR reports, the long-term trend may be rather sharply down, a trend clouded in recent years by variation only cyclical in nature. Thus, in his impressive review of studies of violent crime Gurr (1981) suggests a downward trend running over a century or more in most Western societies with, in the United States, temporary upward surges at roughly fifty-year intervals, starting at about 1860, 1910, and 1960.

The various data sets for the most recent years are confusing but suggest that the upward surge beginning in the 1960s and continuing through the 1970s has come to an end. Thus, the FBI reports (1984:168) from jurisdictions with a total population of 141,692,000 show decreases in index arrests from 1,507,207 in 1980 to 1,486,784 in 1984. Arrests of juveniles from all offenses went from 1,409,768 to 1,255,121 in the same period. Juvenile arrests for index property crimes declined from 500,211 to 410,723 and those for violent index crimes from 63,354 to 54,740. In apparent confirmation of this trend, National Crime Survey data indicate that the proportion of the nation's households touched by crimes of violence or theft has been declining slowly since 1975, with the most rapid decline (to 27 percent from the previous year's 29 percent) occurring between 1982 and 1983, the last years for which data were available at the time of reporting (Bureau of Justice Statistics 1984). The recent past may, then, have seen "crime waves" of some unmeasurable dimension. But to a very real extent, they might be termed "crime reporting waves," as suggested by Galvin and Polk (1982:161). Or, to the extent that they document real phenomena, they may represent almost random ripples rather than major currents within the tides of history.

Unfortunately, an apparent leveling-off in delinquency rates provides no basis for complacency. The baseline from which we started is still high. It is, as far as any available data can tell us, higher than in any country of the Western world. But the data do not demonstrate, as the alarmist would claim, that the behavior of the country's youths is so deteriorating as to suggest that our society has embarked upon a slow, downward slide toward chaos. Quite to the contrary, we might well remember that in Britain, the closest precursor to the United States, the incidence of homicide has dropped by a factor of at least ten since the thirteenth century, that as late as the 1820s it "was worth a prosperous man's life and possessions to venture out at night," and that the few early studies available at least suggest long-term downward trends in personal violence interrupted by periodic waves of serious crime in both England and America (Gurr 1980:412–13, 419). From the point of view of the historian,

> The progress of Western civilization has been marked by increasing internal and external controls on the show of violence. People are socialized to control and displace anger. Norms of conduct in almost all organized activity stress nonviolent means of accomplishing goals. Interpersonal violence within the community and nation is prohibited and subject to sanction in almost all circumstances. The process is in essence a cultural one and like most cultural change had its origins in the changing values of social and intellectual elites. The process, so far as it pertains to violence, contributed not only to the decline in homicide and assault but also to the humanization and rationalization of social policy. It led, for example, to the decline and ultimate abandonment of executions in most Western nations, the end of slavery and the brutalization of wage labor, the passing of corporal punishment in schools and prisons, and many other humane features of contemporary life that are often taken for granted. . . . (Gurr 1981:342)

It is precarious, of course, to predict either the immediate or the long-term future from the past. Since about 1975, some ebbing of delinquency rates seems to have taken place. But it is not certain that the process of "sensitization to violence" of which the historian speaks will continue unabated. The civilizing lesson must be learned anew by each new generation. Certain major upheavals in the past seem to have interrupted temporarily the transmission of the lesson. They may do so again, and their force could be felt very soon.

The most obvious correlate of the great waves of violent crime in the past has been war and postwar readjustment, with its wrenching socioeconomic dislocation, emphasis on unleashed violence, and disillusioning failure to achieve the utopian prospects held out by war leaders as means of enlisting support for supreme endeavor. In England, waves of crime coincided with the successive wars with Spain running from 1739 to 1763 and with the Napoleonic Wars. Lesser increases followed both World Wars. In the United States, the crime peak of the 1860s and 1870s coincided with the turbulence of and following the Civil War, a second high wave came in the decade after World War I, and a third in the post–World War II world, accompanied by the Vietnam War (Gurr 1981:344–45).

We live now in a world marked not only by wars and rumors of wars but in the presence of the threat of the ultimate violence that could destroy civilization. Whether in such presence we find it possible to continue the transmission of the civilizing process remains to be seen.

The present period is also one of widespread concern about a shifting economy and high unemployment, particularly among minority youths. This has led to numerous predictions of rising rates of delinquency and crime. Somewhat surprisingly to many, recent history does not clearly support the expectation. Delinquency seemed to have increased for the 1960–1974 period, generally characterized by relatively high levels of economic prosperity. It seems to have been doing no more than holding steady or, at least as measured by arrests, to have been tapering off since 1974, a period including years of high unemployment and "stagflation." Further available analyses of the past relationships between economic variables and crime are confusing and often seem to come to opposing conclusions. As reviewed and summarized by Gurr (1981:328–33), they show the economic cycle apparently playing a role, but only as a part of constellations of variables that have combined differently in different eras. Thus, some scholars have found property crimes to be related inversely to fluctuations in the economic cycle, but violence to be unrelated or even to vary positively with general economic conditions. Black but not white homicide rates seemed to soar during the prosperous 1960s and early 1970s. Effects of economic variables may be different for different age groups. Thus, while other studies seemed to show little relationship between unemployment and arrest rates in the United States, Daniel Glaser and Kent Rice (quoted by Gurr 1981:329) found high unemployment consistently related to high arrest rates for both property offenses and violent crimes for males in their twenties and thirties, but negatively related to juvenile arrest rates.

The age structure of the population plays an obvious role in relation to delinquency and crime. As young males contribute somewhat disproportionately to overall crime rates, it is not surprising to find an apparent correlation between their numbers and both crime and delinquency. Available data show declining proportions of young people in the population from 1945 to the early 1960s, and sharply increasing proportions from the early 1960s until the early 1970s. Correlations with crime rates seem clear (Gurr 1980:427). However, one may take some comfort from the fact that during the 1980s this situation will change markedly. The country is expected to see an increase of some 10 percent in the population under age 15 between 1980 and 1989, but that aged 15–17 inclusive will decrease by a startling 20 percent and that 18–24 by 15 percent (Freund 1982). If history follows in its own footsteps, this trend should be accompanied by a downturn both in the volume of crime and delinquency and in their rates per 100,000 in the population.

But the extent of any downward trend in rates of crime and delinquency—if indeed, it proceeds at all—will in all probability not be great enough to change the fundamental picture confronting us. American delinquency rates will remain higher than those of other Western societies. They will be sufficiently high as to create enormous unease in our society and to continue to give rise to a pervasive sense that the fabric of social life is deteriorating.

Further, the time is probably past when we can realistically hope that painstaking examination of single factors and their relationship to delinquency rates can either explain variations in such rates, predict them accurately, or lead to an understanding of what should be done about them. Broad behavioral trends are a product of seething interaction within a tangled skein of societal, interpersonal, and intrapersonal variables. We may well be living in a time when the confluence of variables is such as to result in the citizen's diminished willingness to conform to the demands of conventional society. Two World Wars, victories in which produced neither a world "safe for democracy" or the "Four Freedoms" that were promised, a subsequent disastrous foreign war that cost much of our national pride, and succeeding decades of international and civil wars have unleashed on the world a well-publicized pattern of "legitimization of violence" and of resolution of all sorts of human problems through resort to violence. An abandoned "War on Poverty" served only to highlight societal failure to achieve equality of economic opportunity in a world tending to judge the worth of individuals and teaching them to assess their own worth by the degree to which they achieve economic success. Poverty may not cause crime in itself, but frustration and hopelessness accompanying gross relative poverty in a world of apparent abundance may do so.

A president forced to resign in disgrace, legislators revealing themselves in Abscam scandals to be for sale, and constantly renewed revelations of corruption in law enforcement bring a sense that "everybody's doing it" and that our society is one in which "it's every man for himself." Social dislocations resulting from war, from industrialization, and from growing discontent with poverty in the presence of plenty further erode faith in the worth of previously held values.

Neither these nor related factors are subject to precise measurement, nor is their meaning to youths and youths' resultant acceptance or rejection of conforming behavior precisely predictable. One can only conclude that examination of cyclical patterns must be accompanied by examination of the particular forces operating in today's world upon the process of socialization of the young, if more sophisticated assessment of the current social scene is to be achieved.

Who Are Today's Delinquents?

Juvenile crimes may be found in troubling dimensions in all social classes, all races, every socioeconomic level, and all geographic areas. But the hard fact remains that the problem in its overwhelming form is that presented by lower socioeconomic class, minority group males living at the core of the urban area. In 1981, some 86 percent of all index arrests of juveniles for property crimes and almost 90 percent of those for violent crimes were males (FBI 1981:166). This distribution is believed by many to be changing, but the fact remains that between 1972 and 1981 the number of index arrests of juvenile males increased by 32 percent for violent and 22 percent for property crimes, while those for females increased by 26 percent and 23 percent respectively (FBI 1981:166).

The concentration of delinquency in the deteriorated inner-city area has been a phenomenon evident since the studies of Shaw and McKay ([1942] 1969) in the Chicago of the 1920s. Recent studies of such concentration are few, its precise extent is difficult to establish, and it may vary from city to city. Suburban rates may have increased somewhat in recent years. Nonetheless, few students would gainsay the conclusions of the current literature to the effect that serious youth crime in general, and violent youth crime in particular, is far more concentrated in cities of over 250,000 and that in the larger cities it tends to be concentrated in enclaves of high social pathology (Smith et al. 1979:116–18).

The spatial and gender distributions of juvenile crime have long been studied reasonably dispassionately. Not so its racial distribution. To discuss any aspect of race and crime is automatically to give offense and to arouse anger. Thus, the subject has been almost taboo—an "elephant in the room" whose presence one dared not mention. But the stubborn and unwelcome fact of the matter is that delinquency can neither be understood nor meaningfully confronted without grappling with the fact of gross overrepresentation of blacks among both juvenile offenders and their victims. In a recent, not atypical year, blacks composed 14.7 percent of the under-18 population. They contributed 27.2 percent of all index arrests of juveniles for property crime and an even more disproportionate 49.7 percent of those for violent crimes, including 61.6 percent of the arrests for robbery (Shireman 1981:123).

There is no doubt that arrests are not a wholly satisfactory measure of black or any other delinquency. Disparities in arrest rates are often imputed to racist law enforcement resulting in blacks being arrested for crimes that when committed by whites are overlooked. But the data just supplied are those on the serious index crimes only: the crimes most unlikely to be overlooked, no matter who the offender. Further, the people raising this argument tend to be the very ones most likely to declaim (perhaps often justifiably) against inadequate police protection and law enforcement in the black community. Indeed, it is quite probable that if any class of crime is ignored by law enforcement it is crime by blacks against blacks.

It becomes obvious that the problem of crime in the United States cannot be understood unless the nature of the black experience in America is understood. That experience has been different from that of any other racial group. While in the long course of human history, many population groups, representing all races, have been enslaved, blacks were the only group brought to America as slaves, and to most Americans, black or white, "slave" means "black." Just as surely as American blacks have been robbed of pride in their history, they have also been robbed of full recognition of humanness in the present and denied a viable hope for the future. As only one manifestation of this plight, blacks have been locked into inferior jobs or excluded from jobs for generations. In the present, the official unemployment rate for black male youths hovers around 40 percent and would probably be double that in the most disadvantaged central city areas if it were not that large numbers of young black men have given up maintaining contact with the unemployment office and are no longer counted, even among the unemployed.

Poverty alone may not produce crime, and crime rates in general may not fluctuate with the economic cycle. But poverty alongside affluence, in the midst of a culture in which the rhetoric is that of equality of opportunity and accompanied by deep-seated traditions of assumptions of black inferiority, may well produce frustration, rage, and violence. It is difficult to envision anything but continuing and even accelerating rates of black crime and delinquency in the absence of social change making it more readily possible for black youths to move into productive engagement with the economic order. Even if progress toward this end is achieved, it would seem inevitable that we must expect for the years immediately ahead to reap the bitter harvest of a societal condition that has been damaging to the human spirit and has produced a fearful number of badly hurt and therefore hurtful black youths.

CHAPTER 2
THE COUNTERREVOLUTION IN JUVENILE JUSTICE

In the history of the American juvenile justice system, the years from the mid-1960s to the very early 1980s have been a period of counter-revolution. We believe this development to have been necessary and valuable, even inevitable. We also believe that there is danger that it will achieve a powerful momentum, and while sweeping away many of the superficial excrescences and absurdities of the original revolution, may result in the loss of much of value.

As we noted in our introductory chapter, the earlier revolution that ultimately inspired the present reaction had its recent roots in the last half of the nineteenth century. Prior to that time, the prevailing philosophical and value system of the criminal law had largely governed the confrontation between society and the officially identified offender, juvenile or adult. That philosophy rested upon an assumption of free will, within which people are seen as essentially rational beings, choosing their own behavior and responsible for it. The essential role of the criminal law is thus one of determining when violations have taken place and imposing lawfully prescribed sanctions for such violations. The severity of the sanction employed should be proportionate to the gravity of the offense. The prescription by law will place the citizen on notice of the consequence of illegal behavior. Thus obedience to the law and the integrity of the social order will be preserved.

To implement the philosophical system of the law, the criminal justice system has been developed as an elaborately complex and highly sophisticated fact-finding apparatus. In principle, it ensures a process adversary in nature but providing a series of procedures calculated to ensure a fair contest before an impartial tribunal. Over the centuries of their development these procedures have necessarily become ever more complicated, forming a labyrinthine network the penetration of which requires the help of lawyers indoctrinated into the values and trained in the complexities of the system. The whole fabric of assumption, value, law, and operational system has emerged over the centuries as one of the proudest accomplishments of the Anglo-American way of life. It may well be the surest available method of protecting the individual brought before the bar from capricious abuse by the power of the state.

The development of the juvenile court and associated elements of the juvenile justice structure meant that a whole new set of beliefs and values were grafted upon the criminal justice system, rooted in a philosophy of determinism rather than that of free will. The new system was committed to the proposition that juvenile law violation was the natural result of antecedent causes, that such causes often lay in the familial, community, and broader environment to which the child had been exposed, that unfortunate influences arising from such sources could be identified and understood, and that understanding would enable intervention in the child's life and circumstances so that he would no longer need or wish to continue in law-violative behavior. The state, as the ultimate parent of the child, should thus assure that action was taken such as was necessary to heal the hurt child. The prescribed action might be little related to and quite disproportionate to the gravity of the child's offense. But the "social treatment of the whole child" would provide the surest pathway, both to the best welfare of the child and to the ultimate protection of society.

To the present day, the marriage of the child welfare oriented, deterministic philosophy to the longer established personal responsibility model remains one ridden by strife. The juvenile court is in the position of the circus equestrian riding atop two galloping horses, each determinedly striving to go its own way. Our present, perhaps only temporary solution embodies court procedures in two stages. An adjudicatory stage is concerned with the truth of the allegations bringing the child before the court, is largely governed by adversarial judicial and legal concepts, and is subject to classical considerations of due process. If through adjudicatory proceedings charges are sustained, a disposition stage is entered upon. Here the conceptual framework arises from an essentially deterministic view of human nature. The degree to which formal due process procedures, protections against the dangers of judicial discretion, or proportionality between gravity of offense and disposition should obtain remains at issue.

In recent years, it has been frequently asserted that the marriage between legal justice and welfare is a doomed effort to unite incompatible partners and should be dissolved. Thoughtful observers from both sides of the Atlantic have noted that to a still few but perhaps increasing number of scholars "an unashamedly retributionist philosophy underpinning a legally and judicially oriented form of decision making is seen as the most appropriate, and most just, basis for a system of juvenile justice" (Asquith 1983a:5).

But these changes arising from the possible incompatibility of two philosophical systems were not clearly apparent to the founders of the present juvenile justice system. During approximately the last decade of the nineteenth and the first three decades of the twentieth centuries, the philosophy engendered by the "Progressive era" of American social reform led to the development of a whole new "people processing system" for juvenile transgressors. While the function of detection inevitably remained largely a regular police function, once the arrestee was determined to be a juvenile specially selected and trained officers took over and continued police processing from that point. Pretrial detention, when indicated, was no longer to be in the local jail but in a "juvenile detention home," dedicated to the task of representing to the child the benevolent concern of society. Adjudication of allegations concerning the child's illegal behavior, his exposure to criminogenic life influences, or other indications of need for state intervention were the task of the newly created juvenile court, as was the decision as to the course of action to be taken to best protect the child. A new form of service, probation, was in the process of development and was adapted so as to provide surveillance, counsel, and mobilization of needed resources on behalf of the child who was to be returned to the community but was thought to be in need of continued concern on the part of the state. Special "juvenile training schools" were developed in order to remove youths from the degradation of the prisons of the era and to contribute to their reeducation and rehabilitation. Following such care, juveniles were to be returned to the free community under the supervision of and with the guidance and counsel of juvenile "aftercare" or "parole" officers.

By the early part of the twentieth century, a fairly complete framework had been established for the expression of society's official concern for the errant child. It was obvious that the framework remained in many ways skeletal, that resources for the performance of its complicated tasks were often not adequately available, and that frequently it could not achieve its rehabilitative mission. But optimism was high. Growing pains, it was thought, were inevitable. Time would fill in the gaps in knowledge, and the manifest rightness of the course being set would ultimately bring the necessary societal investment in money and energy.

The early widespread acceptance of the philosophy underlying the rehabilitative ideal is attested to by the fact that the juvenile court, the cornerstone of the new system, which first took statutory form in Chicago in 1899, soon became a part of the justice apparatus in almost every state. Further, with surprising rapidity, it spread in a variety of forms to almost every nation of the industrialized world, hailed, for example, by Roscoe Pound, dean of the Harvard Law School, as "the greatest step forward in Anglo-American jurisprudence since the Magna Charta" (Empey 1978:3).

As has been the history of many social innovations, the tide of opinion has largely reversed itself. The recent era is one of insistent criticism of the accomplishments, the methodology, and the philosophy of the juvenile court and its associated instruments. Almost ubiquitous impressions that serious juvenile delinquency was rising and that the country's youths were increasingly "getting out of hand" seemed clearly to indicate that the system had not solved "the delinquency problem." The few studies available on the aftermath of youths' involvement with the court and with "correctional" programs also cast grave doubt on their ability to answer the needs of children who became the system's "clients." In fact, some data seemed to demonstrate that the further into the system young offenders were drawn—and the more, therefore, that they were exposed to its benevolent care—the more likely it was that they would repeat their delinquencies (Wolfgang et al. 1972; Petersilia 1980:366–67). An interminable series of horror stories strongly suggested that the youngster brought before the court was liable to find there neither rehabilitation nor benevolent concern. In fact, he too frequently did not find so much as common decency (Silberman 1978:316 ff). While one could easily muster an equal number of anecdotes of positive justice system intervention in young lives, this hardly served to convince the public either that their protection against "young thugs" was assured or that an adequate response to their sense of outrage and demand for retribution had resulted.

Vociferous attacks upon the juvenile justice system and upon the juvenile court in particular came from both the right and the political and philosophical left. John Conrad captures this tension well:

> On the Right hand, neoconservative critics will insist that the court is administered mainly by puddingheaded judges indifferent to the safety of the public. They will articulate devastating accounts of slovenly decision making in which leniency is granted to those children who least deserve it, with grave dangers to life and property. On the Left hand, some liberals and most radicals are just as certain that the indifference of the juvenile wing of the judiciary is toward the working-class values and concerns of the children appearing in court and of their families. Miscarriages of justice will be cited to show how truants and runaways are sometimes punished more harshly than young thieves and thugs. (Conrad 1981:544)

The resultant crisis in general public confidence has been heightened by the fact that within the ranks of two scholarly disciplines particularly concerned with the juvenile court—the legal profession and the academic social sciences, particularly sociology—there had long existed strong ambivalence about the philosophy, underlying assumptions, and methodology of contemporary juvenile justice practice. Many or most of the scholarly analyses of the juvenile justice system have tended to start with the assumption that its failures are not merely those of any social institution struggling with sparse resources to cope with an overwhelming problem, but are failures in basic principle.

The present need, it seems apparent to us, is to break out of the current confused mixture of despair, pragmatism, and optimism. We are impressed by the selection by Justice David Bazelon, one of today's most eminent legal practitioner-scholars, of a quotation from John Conrad, a major correctional practitioner-philosopher: "More than most human institutions, corrections needs a vision to work toward. . . . The first step toward the attainment of that vision is to reopen the dialogue upon the great issues" (Conrad 1981:ix). Our endeavor is to take some few small steps toward furthering dialogue upon at least some of the issues that must be resolved if juvenile justice is to achieve "a vision to work toward." We focus first on issues derived most immediately from the legal tradition. Next, we turn to those brought forward by the sociological perspective.

"Due Process," Diminished Responsibility, and Societal Protection

As the early optimism about the juvenile court's capacities to accomplish its mission of curing began to fade, the first efforts of the revisionists were directed at remedying the court's procedures, fashioned to give it the greatest possible opportunity to exercise a quasi-parental function with respect to the child. It had become evident to many that in the court's use of authority presumably to do domething *for* the child, it was inevitable that something be done *to* the child. Too often frustrated in attempts to cure, the court could readily turn to the imposition of restrictions. Often this meant the incarceration of youths in settings uncomfortably reminiscent of prisons. And, it seemed evident, if this happened to only a few, all youths subject to the threat of loss of freedom should be accorded the protections against abuse of authority by the state guaranteed in the Constitution to all persons whose liberty is at stake in judicial proceedings.

The decade from the mid-1960s to the mid-1970s saw enormous progress toward recognition that, as Mr. Justice Fortas proclaimed in the landmark *In Re Gault* (1966), "neither the Fourteenth Amendment nor the Bill of Rights is for adults alone." By contrast, earlier positions had often been governed by beliefs such as that stated in an often-quoted Pennslvania appellate court decision: "To save a child from becoming a criminal . . . the Legislature may surely provide for the salvation of such child, if its parents or guardian be unable or unwilling to do so, by bringing it into one of the courts of the state without any process at all" *(Commonwealth v. Fisher, 1905)*. With Gault, it became clear that in juvenile court proceedings in which subjects are at risk of commitment to institutions for delinquents, they are entitled, *during that part of court proceedings devoted to the adjudication of facts,* to many of the traditional protections of the criminal law. Specifically ensured were the rights to notice of specific charges, notice of right to counsel, right to confront and cross-examine witnesses, and protection against self-incrimination.

In 1972, in its *In Re Winship,* the Supreme Court further held that charges of criminal law violation must be proved beyond a reasonable doubt, just as in criminal court. In its 1975 ruling in *Breed v. Jones,* the same court held that a child earlier adjudicated on a delinquency charge in juvenile court would be placed in unconstitutional double jeopardy if the charge were readjudicated in criminal court. Even before *Gault,* it had been ruled in *Kent v. United States* (1966), the first juvenile court case ever to be accepted and considered by the Supreme Court, that juveniles subject to juvenile court jurisdiction could not be waived to criminal court without a hearing and without due process.

By the early 1970s, then, much had been accomplished in defining the protections available to the child as the court went about weighing the facts of the charges against him and determining whether or not his behavior was such as to bring him within the jurisdiction of the state. A conceptual base for the provision of due process to juveniles had been fairly well developed and had been affirmed by legal precedent. True, implementation often lagged—some juvenile court judges and many court officials remain prone to advising the juvenile and his family of their constitutional rights in so perfunctory a manner as to be almost unintelligible. Overwhelmed and often not too interested, "counsel" may be appointed only five minutes before a court hearing and have even less time to review the file and meet the client. Issues regarding some rights afforded adult offenders—the right to jury trial, to public trial, and to bail, for example—remain largely unresolved. Nonetheless, in major areas formerly at dispute, precedent has been established and principles are fairly generally accepted. The remaining problems in these areas are primarily those of implementation, just as they are in many other courts. No compelling reason would appear to make them less susceptible of solution in juvenile than in criminal court.

Unfortunately, success in bringing due process into the juvenile court's jurisdictional hearing does not necessarily ensure the child fairness in ultimate treatment. Important though the victories in moving toward procedural due process have been, they do not reach to the possibly more substantive question of what should be done once state jurisdiction is assumed. The danger is in becoming so engrossed with procedural issues in ruling, for example, whether the youngster actually stole the car that the usually much more complex issue of what is to be done with him once he has been found to have done so is barely considered.

Perhaps in part because of its awesome complexity, and in part because it brings into play a "child welfare" rather than a "free will" philosophy, this last question has failed to engage the active interest of legal scholars to the extent that the earlier struggle for procedural due process did. The full lesson of Gerald Gault's court experience is seldom drawn. Gerald was accused of making salacious telephone calls to an older woman. Had he been an adult, his offense could have resulted in a fine of not more than fifty dollars or a jail term of up to two months. But after a hearing grossly wanting in protection of due process (proper notice was not given, charges were specified in only the vaguest ways, hearsay testimony was admitted with neither Gerald nor his parents being accorded the right of cross-examination and rebuttal, not the slightest gesture toward provision of counsel was made), Gerald was committed at age 15 to a state institution until his twenty-first birthday unless earlier released at the initiative of the institution. The entire procedure was shocking, illustrative though it was of entirely too frequent juvenile court abuse of due process. *But is is rarely observed that it is quite possible that exactly the same disposition of Gerald's case might have been made following an adjudicatory hearing including all the traditional due process protections.* Such disposition would probably have resulted in very little outcry. After all, a large proportion of the population of the nation's juvenile correctional institutions at the time was made up of "status offenders," convicted of behaviors that are legal offenses only when committed by children: truancy, running away, being ungovernable, and similar acts even less "criminal" than was Gerald's.

We are here suggesting that the last decade's accomplishments represent only opening skirmishes rather than victories in the battle for justice for the child. It is in the ultimate disposition and treatment of the child that the fundamental issues of the substance and purpose of the juvenile court and the associated elements of the juvenile justice system lie.

The Issue of Responsibility

As we have noted, at the very core of the Anglo-American legal tradition is the assumption that behavior is the product of volition. From this assumption, the state may—indeed, must—hold the citizen to legally prescribed behavioral standards through the application of sanctions for misbehavior. Such sanctions should vary in severity in proportion to the severity of the offense, and should result only from violations of existing law. Thus the citizen is provided with fair warning of what conduct is prohibited and of the consequences of violations.

But lawyers entering the world of the juvenile court often find themselves in an unfamiliar arena. The juvenile's conduct is often seen as the natural result of causes many of which lie outside his control. Thus, his law-violative behavior may be perceived as calling not for sanctions but for helpful intervention in its presumed causes. The juvenile justice system's response to delinquency may be quite disproportionate to the severity of any particular offense. Persons brought before the court for seemingly identical conduct may receive widely differing treatment.

At the heart of the matter lies the legal concept of the "diminished responsibility" of the child. Bearing such diminished responsibility, the juvenile is considered to merit the justice system's more helping, less punitive approach. But it has proven enormously difficult to define just how, to what degree, and extending to what developmental stage, such "diminishment" should be presumed to exist. The concept remains so cloudy as to be rendered vulnerable in an era marked by general fear and resentment of the young offender. The juvenile court is currently under bitter attack as being too prone to treat dangerous "toughs" as innocents; hence, the decline of "child saving." One policeman expressed this clearly in an interview with a distinguished investigator: "The law says a kid should be treated differently because he can be rehabilitated, but they weren't robbing, killing, and raping when kiddie court was established. Kids are different now, but the law hasn't caught up with the changes" (Silberman 1978:311).

Yet, the juvenile court does operate as a part of the mechanism established to deal with behaviors that society refuses to tolerate. The court has the responsibility not *only* to serve the welfare of the child but also to protect society. To accomplish this last function, it is armed with much the same coercive powers as the criminal court and it operates as a wing of the criminal justice system.

To the legalist—and to the person on the street, or to the state legislator, as well—it often appears that in recent decades the juvenile court has tended to disregard its responsibility to protect society from the continued, frequently very serious misdeeds of the young. At least some foundation in reality for that belief must be granted. The court's actions often do not seem to implement the necessary function of providing to young people warning of prohibited behavior and of the consequences of violation. Critics have no difficulty in discovering evidence of court dispositions seeming to obscure for the young person any connection between behavior and consequences.

Typical have been the observations of police and state's attorneys in the state of Washington, in the past considered to be far advanced in its pursuit of the rehabilitative ideal. Strong reaction to that philosophy has long been simmering. An official of the Seattle Police Department recites readily available stories of juveniles committing crime with impunity. He recalls, "We had a kid who had been arrested 64 times, 35 of them for felonies. And he had never done time in an institution" (Serrill 1980:37). While this case may be a shocking extreme (and while there is probably much more to the story than the quotation reveals), teenagers committed to institutions in the state had been convicted of an average 7.5 felonies before commitment (ibid:40)—and in almost all jurisdictions even a first conviction has most frequently been preceded by a series of police contacts resulting in warnings and/or informal dispositions by police and courts.

Studies in other states reveal similar patterns. In one of the most careful of those, in Columbus, Ohio, dispositional patterns resulting from almost 5,000 offenses committed by 1,138 violent juvenile offenders were examined. Such variables as nature of offense and prior record yielded predictions of disposition little more accurate than would "tossing coins in the courtroom" (Hamparian et al. 1978:114).

Such a situation cannot be expected to demonstrate to youths the logical consequences of behavior. Indeed, the young person who may have violated the law several times without being caught, who for several violations that have been brought to official attention has received only a dismissal, a warning that some day serious consequences may follow if he continues his behavior, or has received nominal probation, can only perceive either that the social order and the state are not actually much concerned about his behavior or that they are simply ineffectual—or both. There is danger that when, finally, the repeat offender does encounter firm treatment in the form of correctional placement, the sanction will be perceived as almost random, as "bad luck," or as discrimination—perhaps an occasion for deciding to "get even," but hardly an occasion for reform.

The origins of patterns of what may be perceived as unrealistic leniency followed by sharp sanctions are not hard to discern. Juvenile court judges and court officers spend their professional lives in brief encounters with seriously delinquent juveniles—several thousand of them a year in the big city courts where the problem is most acute. Judges, in particular, encounter such youngsters in settings removed from the day-to-day world of the street. Over and over again, they read reports of violative behavior and briefly confront its perpetrators—but only rarely do they encounter the persons who have been injured by it. It is possible that perspective may be lost. Offenses seeming to the public, and especially to injured parties, to be monstrous come to seem almost commonplace.

Even more determinative is the fact that, over and over again, the court must make *some* case disposition. To some youths, the experiences of arrest, perhaps temporary detention pending court hearing, and court appearance are meaningful in themselves and will serve as a deterrent. But for the more seriously and persistently delinquent, available dispositional choices, in their actual form if not their rhetoric, are often only two. The first is return of the offender to the community and to the streets from which he came. This may be accompanied by an admonitory lecture from a judge who seems to the juvenile to come from a different world, and/or a warning of a possible future consequence the juvenile only vaguely perceives. A community disposition can include probation, which to some youths can mean surveillance, counseling, and mustering of any available services needed, but often may be only nominal. Any such disposition may seem to the youth almost less meaningful than a slap on the wrist. But the only other available alternative is too often commitment to a "training school" well known to the court to do very little positive "training." The gap between almost meaningless reaction and harmful overreaction is of Grand Canyon dimensions.

The problem is real, it is significant, and it is enormously complex. It demands a social policy response. But the responses most commonly, often vigorously urged tend to be simplistic in nature and to arise from frustration rather than reasoned calculation of probable results. They differ in detail, but are essentially of two sorts. The first would seek abandonment of the whole juvenile court idea and return of all juvenile offenders to criminal court "where they will be assured the protections of due process." The second, more frequently and perhaps somewhat more cogently advocated response is represented by a series of proposals that would retain a juvenile court of sorts but would either limit its jurisdiction or curb its discretion over "nuisance" and over very serious offenders, particularly those charged with violent crimes against persons.

The Abolitionist Extreme

Those who would abolish the juvenile court most frequently rest their argument on the premise that a necessary and desirable shift toward holding youths responsible for their misdeeds is under way. This, they say, is more consistent with the traditions and ideology of the criminal court. If youths are to be punished for their law violations, penalties should be imposed by a judicial body that admits in a straightforward way that the goal is punishment, rather than one retreating to a screen of euphemistic language about treatment. Trial in a criminal court would permit the juvenile's attorney to function in an adversarial role and thus to more adequately further the youth's interests than does a nonadversary proceeding operating under the dubious assumption that all parties are dedicated to promoting the "best interest of the child."

To us, the proposals of the juvenile court "abolitionists" do not appear responsive to the very real problems confronting the juvenile justice system today. Simply shifting the arena in which problems are to be engaged would seem to promise little of value. Further, as we shall shortly argue at greater length, we do not agree with the abolitionists' assumption that our citizenry and our policymakers are ready to abandon completely the concept of a court expressing society's intent to intervene constructively on the behalf of the juvenile whose personality and attitudes toward society's demands are still in the process of formation. We are quite aware that an essential component of intervention must usually be a firm confrontation of the juvenile with the wrongness of his behavior and with its possible consequences. But we also believe that our society continues to expect that confrontation should often be only a part of a necessary response, and that our orientation should also be to the factors contributing to the juvenile's failure to conform in the first place.

That the court's intervention in the lives of juveniles accused of offenses should be governed by traditional considerations of due process and fairness seems to us self-evident. But we see no reason to believe that fairness may not be achieved in a court in which a juvenile is properly represented by counsel and in which the constitutional guarantees are decreed. It is difficult for us to perceive how the abolitionist position can appeal to anyone giving thoughtful consideration to the actual practices, rather than the ideal model, of criminal justice in the United States. In particular, one must recall that if juvenile court were abolished, most juveniles now brought before it become the concern of misdemeanant courts and their associated police lockups and local jails—the system so long considered the disgrace of the American justice system.

To us, then, the abolitionist's position seems only a distant muttering of thunder on the horizon. We believe that it will not develop further—particularly if pathways to more constructive solutions are vigorously explored.

A Narrowed Juvenile Court?

A much more real possibility is considerable expansion of the present, fairly frequent moves to retain the juvenile court but narrow its function. This would be done either by removing specified juvenile offender groups from the court's jurisdiction or by limiting its discretion by imposing statutorily mandated sentences for designated offenses. Almost all students of the problem concede that there are some juveniles whose offenses and offense records are so indicative of continuing danger to citizens, or call for such strong societal condemnation, as to necessitate the imposition of state control for longer periods than those available to most juvenile courts. Some sort of provision for criminal court trial of such youths is made in all states. But the issue coming to the fore today is, "Who decides?" Who is to decide, by what process, which youths are to be tried in criminal rather than juvenile court?

By far the most common path by which juveniles reach criminal court is that of juvenile court waiver of jurisdiction. In this pattern, original jurisdiction is with the juvenile court. That court may, by due process of law, find in individual instances that jurisdiction should be waived to criminal court.

There are, however, two other answers to the "Who decides?" question. In some states, the legislature has retained this prerogative. Statutorily defined classes of offenders—all those above specified ages accused of designated offenses, for example—automatically appear in criminal court. Examples would include New York's elimination of juvenile court jurisdiction over all persons over age 16 or Delaware's exclusion of murder from juvenile court jurisdiction.

In other states, the legislature delegates to the prosecutor, or to some agent other than the juvenile court, the authority to decide whether juveniles of specified ages and accused of specified crimes should be tried as adults. Perhaps the major example of this arrangement is the 1978 New York law mandating original criminal court jurisdiction for juveniles of ages as low as 13 accused of any of a wide range of offenses, including burglary, a term which when applied to juveniles may cover a wide range of behaviors. The criminal court may then "waive down" to juvenile court youths found by it to be suitable candidates for juvenile jurisdiction.

Statutorily imposed mandatory sentencing for specific offenses represents another pathway to the curbing of juvenile court discretion. In Washington state, for example, most sentences are dictated by a "sentencing grid" that combines nature of offense and past offense record into combinations specifying disposition. In Illinois, sentencing to the state Department of Corrections, without eligibility for parole, for a period running to the twenty-first birthday, is mandated for all youths convicted of a range of designated offenses and having been twice convicted of prior felony offenses. (One wonders whether the legislators enacting this statute could possibly have realized that they were mandating sentences automatically harsher for younger than for older juveniles.) California and Colorado are among other states having enacted statutes mandating or establishing strong presumption of incarceration for specified classes of juveniles.

The various state laws curbing the discretion or the jurisdiction of the juvenile court are of recent origin. Little hard data evaluating them is available—and, generally, little attempt is made to generate them. Still, some data suggesting a few still-tentative but impressive conclusions about the operation of the new laws have been published. One study report presents the following summary of the results of the New York law: of every 100 arrests for offenses covered by the law, only 23 result in indictment, 12 in criminal convictions, and 6 in adult criminal court sentences, only 2 of which are for periods exceeding the powers of the family (juvenile) court. Cases originating in adult court under the new law are often "waived down" to juvenile court—and, ironically, youths tried in that court, where offenses tend to be less serious, are more likely to be committed to a secure facility than are youths tried in adult court (Howell and Allen-Hagen 1982:29).

Other observers point out that, as might have been predicted, the New York law has not eliminated discretion in the handling of serious youthful offenders—it has merely located discretion with the police and prosecutors who may determine the nature of the charges to be filed, often as the result of a plea-bargaining process. And, as is common in the country's criminal courts, it has produced case backlogs, delay, and lengthier pretrial secure detention (Fisher et al., quoted by Fagan et al. 1981:44).

Available bits of data on the California experience resemble those from New York. In Los Angeles, the new legislation produced a three-fold increase in waivers to adult court. Approximately 20 percent of those waived did not go to trial. Of those tried and convicted, 58 percent did not receive adult type confinements (Howell and Allen-Hagen 1982). The imposition of sanction may well be more likely in juvenile court!

Generally, then, we consider these and similar enactments automatically shifting whole classes of juveniles to the jurisdiction of the criminal court to be ill-considered and overly simplistic reactions to a complex problem. They have political appeal in that they both suggest that something is being done and promise punishment of some juveniles who have aroused community outrage. But the thrust to take action about a problem should best be accompanied by careful calculation of the probability that the proposed action will lead to a desired result. The presently advocated automatic transfer laws can accomplish little to increase security of the citizen, to reduce the volume of delinquency, or to achieve justice either for the offender or for his victim. Indeed, their unintended consequence may well impede the achievement of these goals. Such would seem to be the lessons to be derived from the observations available concerning their application to date, as well as from their lack of theoretical bases for a more positive result.

The core of the problem is the assumption that the juvenile is completely described, for the purpose of making decisions so momentous to his life and to the community of which he is a member, by placing him within a narrow range of offense group classifications: he is a "burglar" or an "assaulter," for example, and only that. This assumption may be comforting to many framers of criminal law, but it is arrant nonsense when rigidly applied in practice. One way or another, in disposing of offense cases a wide range of variables other than offense class must and will be taken into consideration. Among such variables will be the gravity of the actual violation, the maturity of the individual, his role in relation to other participants in the offense, the social pressures under which he was operating, and his broader familial, school, and community adjustment. Prosecutorial discretion, exercised through reduction of charge, plea bargaining, or other available recourse, provides a channel for individualized decision making that will be followed for want of another. Court or jury refusal to make guilty findings constitute other channels. Variation in police filing is another. But these paths, honestly presented, would find little acceptance. They are no more than unintended latent consequences of the closing off of other alternatives.

We have previously noted our conviction that *some* juveniles do exist who are so "mature," present such danger to the community, or have committed offenses that so arouse societal condemnation as to necessitate their transfer to adult court. But it appears to us that the complicated range of issues involved in determining which youths meet this description necessitates an openly arrived at decision following prescribed due process. It should be made by a court committed to the propositions that juveniles are juveniles, that they often differ from adults, and that public policy decrees that in all but exceptional cases they are to be dealt with in a court attuned to the needs of juveniles and to the societal problems posed by juveniles. That court should also be thoroughly conversant with the capacities and resources of juvenile justice and related educational, social service, health, and other pertinent societal systems. Quite obviously, we refer to the juvenile court. We support the studied recommendation of the Institute of

Judicial Administration–American Bar Association Joint Commission on Juvenile Justice Standards, made after considerable deliberation:

    a. The juvenile court should have original and exclusive jurisdiction over juveniles committing offenses while fifteen years of age or younger.

    b. The criminal court should achieve jurisdiction over offenders sixteen or seventeen years of age only if the juvenile court has waived its jurisdiction. (IJA-ABA 1977:15–19)

We are aware that if the IJA-ABA recommendation is to govern, it will be necessary in many ways for the American juvenile court to better develop its capacities to deal with the serious offender. We shall later suggest some of the ways in which it appears to us that this must be done. A wholly satisfactory system will not emerge, however. The problem is of such complexity and human fallibility is so inevitable that blunders will occur under any system. We strive for the least unsatisfactory system humanly available. The achievement of even that limited goal would be momentous.

"Labeling" and the Justice System

It is not only from the legal tradition that fundamental questions arise concerning the philosophy and practice of the juvenile court. Questions are also thrust to the fore by certain assumptions long influential in the field of sociology. In recent years attacks in principle upon the concept of positive intervention have come most often from the body of sociological theory referred to as "labeling theory." Labeling theorists have typically held that "crime" and "delinquency" are constructs of society, and that in fabricating such concepts society inevitably fabricates the criminal or delinquent. The major, though to large extent latent function of the criminal and juvenile justice system's operations is the labeling and thus stigmatization of those brought within their networks. Those so labeled achieve both a public reputation and a private self-concept defining them as "different," as inferior, and as not properly members of conventional society.

The heart of the labeling theorist's position was early (1938) defined by Frank Tannenbaum, one of the founders of contemporary sociological study of crime. In one of the most often quoted statements ever emerging from the criminological literature, he propounded that

> The process of making the criminal, therefore, is a process of tagging, defining, identifying, segregating, describing, emphasizing, making conscious and self-conscious; it becomes a way of stimulating, suggesting, emphasizing and evoking the very traits that are complained of. If the theory of relation of response to stimulus has any meaning, the entire process of dealing with the young delinquent is mischievous insofar as it identifies him to himself or to the environment as a delinquent person.
>
> The person becomes the thing he is described as being. Nor does it seem to matter whether the valuation is made by those who would punish or by those who would reform. . . . Their [those who would reform] very enthusiasm defeats their aim. The harder they work to reform evil, the greater the evil grows under their hands. . . . The way out is through a refusal to dramatize the evil. The less said about it the better. (Tannenbaum [1938] 1951:19–20)

Although Tannenbaum's writings gained him many academic followers, his views on labeling probably had little impact upon social policy until the 1960s, a time of postwar disillusionment, breakdown of faith in established beliefs, hopes, and ways, and, in particular, cynicism about the capacity of the state to intervene positively in human affairs. The times prepared a fertile field for theories emphasizing the innocence of human beings until entrapped by a corrupting society. Labeling theory provided a theoretical foundation for at least a part of the era's pervasive though inchoate sense of protest. Such works as Becker's *Outsiders* (1963) gained enormous prestige. In particular, the pessimistic view of the juvenile court expressed in Edwin Lemert's 1967 essay, prepared for the report of the U.S. President's Commission on Law Enforcement and the Administration of Justice (Lemert 1967), contributed to the shaping of that commission's findings and recommendations.

In turn, the President's Commission's report, expressing so well the ethos of the times, contributed powerfully to the development of federal policy regarding the juvenile and criminal justice systems. That policy, expressed through massive grant-in-aid programs, had among its key-stones the famous "Four Ds" we discussed in our introductory chapter: decriminalization, diversion, due process, and deinstitutionalization.

To very real degree, then, the President's Commission and subsequent federal policy expressed fear of the possible criminogenic effect of over-use of the sanctioning system of the law as it applied to juveniles. They appear to have acknowledged a danger inherent in the labeling process. *But they did not assume that the sole, the overwhelming, or the inevit-able effect of exposure to the justice system was criminogenic.* They left in place both the juvenile court and the concept of positive intervention by the state in the life of the offender.

The remaining question, of course, is how far to go in tailoring juve-nile justice practice and policy to the dangers of state intervention per-ceived by the labeling theorists. The theorists would go much further than is suggested by federal policy generally supporting decriminaliza-tion, diversion, due process, and deinstitutionalization but also support-ing the concept of benign state intervention. More typical of the label-ing theorists' position is, for example, Edwin Schur's (1973) influential call for a policy of "radical nonintervention" and "benign neglect" as a proper response to all but severely antisocial acts, such acts to result in official action embodying "increased formalization of whatever juvenile court procedures remain" (p. 23), and in forthrightly punitive treat-ment. The rather considerable group of "radical criminologists," strongly influenced by Marxist ideology, adds another dimension to the argument, with their perception of the entire criminal and juvenile jus-tice systems as functioning almost solely to perpetuate the subjection of oppressed classes. Thus, for example, Anthony Platt (1977), in *The Child Savers: The Invention of Delinquency,* almost completely rewrites the history of the juvenile court, portraying the motives of its founders and its continued existence as arising almost exclusively from a need to maintain the security of wealth and privilege (see the refutation of Platt's argument by Schultz 1973).

The present necessity seems to us to be for objective assessment of the degree to which social policy should rest upon the labeling theorists' assumptions that the most powerful result of exposure to the juvenile justice system is a labeling process that is inevitably criminogenic.

As we attempt the necessary assessment, we would first note that labeling theory applied to the functioning of the juvenile justice system is pervasive in its intuitive appeal—but that thus far it has been impossible to develop empirical demonstrations of its validity. Experimental random assignment of humans to two groups, one "labeled" and one "not labeled" is, of course, impossible. Attempts to find or interpret existing statistical data to prove a "labeling effect" have been unavailing. Theorists at one point made much of the findings of self-report studies of samples of American youths showing that most—or almost all—young people engage in at least some delinquent behavior at some time during their adolescence or childhood. Thus, it was argued, all youths *could* be labeled delinquent—the only difference between them was that this had officially been done to some and not to others; that is, some had been apprehended and processed through the justice system while others had not. Thus, "those who become officially known as criminals are merely a biased sample of persons who commit crimes selected to fulfill a scapegoat function" (Doleschal and Klapmuts 1973:610).

The situation may not be so simple, however. As Hirschi (1980: 278–91) cogently points out, statements such as the foregoing are true only if it can be assumed that almost all children are identical with respect to engaging in law-violative behavior, the only difference being that some are caught. This is a naive assumption. The self-report and other studies show only that most youths have engaged in *some* law-violative behavior—*but some much more frequently and seriously than others.* The members of this last group are more likely than others to be apprehended, processed, and labeled *by virtue of the fact that it is they who commit the many and the serious delinquent acts.* The behavior, then, preceded the label.

The possibility exists, of course, that the label, once achieved, may be among the factors contributing to the continuation or aggravation of delinquent behavior. But admission that this may be so by no means constitutes admission either that the label created the delinquent or that the label is the inevitable or even the primary factor contributing to continuation or aggravation.

Again as noted by Hirschi (1980), those seeking to verify the labeling proposition empirically have had recourse to data purporting to demonstrate systematic bias on the part of the decision makers—police, courts, and others—who determine which offenders are to receive sanctions and which not. The argument here is that systematic bias results in youngsters having committed similar acts receiving different dispositions. Thus youths who are poor, who are members of minority groups, or who are in other ways disadvantaged are most likely to be channeled into the juvenile justice system and to receive punitive dispositions—guilty findings, out-of-home placement, etc. Such dispositions then result in further delinquency—classically, the label creates the problem.

Acceptance of this position rests upon acceptance of two prior assumptions: first, that the dispositional process actually is systematically biased, and second, that more severe sanctions inevitably result in the aggravaton of offense behavior. Neither propositon can be clearly demonstrated.

The studies of some scholars do seem to point to factors such as ethnicity, social class, or other nonlegal factors tending to produce differing dispositions for youths charged with similar offenses and having similar offense records (Cicourel 1968; Piliavin and Briar 1964; Thornberry 1973). However, a series of at least equally rigorous studies tend to demonstrate that police and juvenile court procedures are influenced primarily by the nature and seriousness of the offense and the previous offense record (Black and Reiss 1970; Terry 1967; Cohen and Klugel 1978; and numerous others).

The situation seems equally cloudy as regards the assumption that the more severe sanctions automatically result in the aggravation of offense behavior. Dramatic demonstrations that harsh sanctions do not result in the termination of violative behavior have long existed and continue to multiply (Wolfgang et al. 1972; Hamparian et al. 1978; Haapanen and Jesness 1982; and numerous others). But empirical demonstration that labeling followed by intervention is a universal, necessary, or major *cause* of continued or aggravated violative behavior is difficult to generate (Mahoney 1974).

We consider the extremes of both the labeling and the antilabeling position to be products of obscured vision resulting from preoccupation with ideology. We do not at all doubt that in some jurisdictions some minority-group and socioeconomically deprived youths receive dispositions more severe than those generally accorded nonminority youths from more advantaged backgrounds. We suspect that such result might often ensue in situations in which courts can uncover no alternative but a justice system disposition for minority youngsters from deprived areas, while families and others may be more readily capable of bringing forward appealing and appropriate nonjustice-system alternatives for more advantaged youths. We are aware that discriminating treatment may sometimes result from sheer bigotry. But we are also aware that as a result of a probably invidious form of selective police attention—or inattention—much behavior that would result in arrest in middle-class areas is never brought to official notice in the deprived inner-city neighborhood. Further, our personal observations, plus the studies of others (Black and Reiss 1970:74) suggest that very often the police and courts are vigorous in thrusting delinquents *out* of the system (and that they are frequently subjected to severe public criticism as a result).

In short, we do not find particularly convincing conclusions about "the police" or "American juvenile justice" based upon studies of tiny, nonrandom samples of the operations of those enormously complex and disparate institutions—studies in which it is impossible to control for wide ranges of possibly intervening variables and from which, therefore only the most tenuous inferences as to causal relationships may be drawn.

We further note that attempts to observe "labeling effects" in juvenile justice directly, instead of inferring their existence from other data, are rare. One that we did encounter was Foster's (1972) study of two samples of institutionalized delinquent boys, in which it proved impossible to discern that the boys perceived any negative stigma resulting from their justice system experience, either in terms of relationship with family, friends, or teachers or in terms of limitations on education or employment.

On the other hand, we do not agree with those who would apparently deny that selection for labeling, justice system disposition, and sanctioning may for some youngsters exert a powerful pressure toward continued violative behavior. The adolescent saying "I've got the name, so I might as well have the game," long antedates the studies of labeling theorists. No practitioner with long experience in helping reintroduce youths who have left institutions to school will have failed to encounter teachers and principals making their return difficult—as well as many who offer unflagging help. Both as scholars and as practitioners, we have encountered the "school for crime" aspect of the correctional institution. But we have also known youngsters who have found in certain institutions help in achieving new perceptions of themselves and their relationships to the world about them, who have left determined to take up life anew, in more positive ways. (We have seen some of these last youngsters make it on the outside and others fail, usually because of familial, community, or other barriers having little to do with the correctional experience—barriers that defeated them before and did so again upon their discharge from the correctional system.)

In sum, we do not believe that the currently necessary rethinking of juvenile justice policy and practice should begin with the assumption that the system is necessarily criminogenic and that positive interventions are inherently invidious. We believe that there is risk involved. Employed indiscriminately, the juvenile justice experience may prove more handicapping than helpful to many of those undergoing it, although the experience is usually contributive to rather than determinative of future behavior. We also believe that we almost invariably lack the means of determining in advance how a multifaceted juvenile justice experience will combine with a myriad of personal and situational factors to determine outcome. Thus, we do not believe that it is possible to justify coercive intervention in the life of the offender in order to "help" or "rehabilitate" him. But there are numerous grounds other than rehabilitation for coercive intervention in the lives of offenders—and if intervention does become necessary, we most certainly believe that it should be accompanied by the offer of the most assiduous and skilled help in coping with the problems contributing to violative behavior. This point we shall expand upon in subsequent chapters.

CHAPTER 3
TANGLED PATHWAYS TO THE FUTURE: ISSUES OF ROLE AND FUNCTION

We have stated our fundamental rejection of the arguments of those who would abolish the juvenile court, those who would eliminate its jurisdiction over large, statutorily defined classes of serious juvenile offenders, and those who contend that the juvenile justice process itself is inevitably a factor in the generation of violative behavior. But rejection of the proposals of others is not an adequate response. We are aware of the critic's responsibility to contribute positively to the present dialogue. This we endeavor to do, in the conviction that the pressing necessity is to provide a sound base for that dialogue by calling attention to the "great issues" underlying current debate. First among these issues, in our opinion, is the definition of the role of the state in a democratic society vis-a-vis the juvenile offender. Springing from that issue is one of the fundamental function and purpose that the juvenile justice system is designed to serve. We are quite aware of the existence of numerous operational questions seeming important to many: for example, methods of selection of judges, "family" versus "juvenile" courts, judicial versus executive branch administration of probation and detention, various pathways to the training of probation and other correctional system staff, and many others. But we are convinced that the many pressing problems at these levels must be resolved in the light of prior considerations of value and social function.

The Reduced Responsibility of the Juvenile

Much of our analysis is premised upon the assumption that there continues to exist in our society a fairly wide consensus that juveniles do tend to differ from adults and that special provision must be made for them apart from the adult criminal law. The consensus is not complete, of course. Statements to the effect that "If they commit adult crimes they should be treated as adults" are common. As with almost all truly significant issues, universal agreement will never be achieved. But both law and social custom have long taken cognizance of fairly widely shared belief that the young person is not yet wholly formed, is in the process of developing, and must be treated so as to promote to the degree possible reintegration rather than permanent alienation from the society about him.

The differing needs and capacities of juveniles and adults have long been recognized in many areas of social living. Particular restrictions are placed upon juveniles' rights to vote, to marry, to consume alcohol, to drive automobiles, to engage in designated occupations, and in many other ways to function as adults. We should probably examine more frequently the basis for our recognition of the reduced capacities of juveniles in these areas of life as well as in our confrontation with the juvenile offender. Thus, beliefs are widely shared that

1. Juveniles characteristically have less capacity than do adults to reckon the results and costs to themselves or to others of their own behavior. Thus, it is inevitable that many aspects of their behavior will seem to the adult impulsive, short-sighted, and irresponsible. As a result, juveniles willl frequently need external help and controls, but the need does not necessarily suggest "viciousness," fundamental difference from others, or need for long-term isolation from society. Fortunately, "juvenileness" is, for most, a transitory state.

2. Childhood and youth are periods of experimentation, of ambivalence, of trying out and discarding various often widely divergent self-concepts and values. The impulsively self-centered and destructive young person of today may be the young idealist of tomorrow—and vice versa.

3. Normal adolescent social development includes a considerable component of establishing one's identity as a self separate from adults and, most especially, separate from dependence upon and control by parents and those associated with parents. This process often involves a degree of rejection of conventional values and an assertion of the right and necessity of forming one's own. The greater the adolescent's inner fear of immaturity, the more aggressive his protest of self-sufficiency is likely to be.

4. The offense behaviors of juveniles are more frequently and more evidently than those of adults immediate outgrowths of family, community, and societal breakdown. The most hurtful youngster is generally the one who has been most hurt. Thus, to the concept of individual guilt must be added that of a widely shared, societal guilt. Intervention in the course of the juvenile's misbehavior will often necessitate countering the damage being done to him.

These considerations do not suggest that "there's no such thing" as a bad boy or girl. Indeed, they tend both to confirm and to explain the facts that serious, sometimes repetitive, not infrequently violent juvenile violations are not uncommon. It is the responsibility of the state to take all feasible steps to protect the citizen from such behavior. But our understanding of the nature of "juvenileness" also dictates that repressive measures are not enough. Our stance must include recognition of the societal stake in the future citizen and of the fact that human beings, particularly young ones, do grow and change. With very rare exceptions, juvenile offenders will eventually return to the free community, there to live long lives. The public interest, as well as the interest of the youths involved, dictates that decisions affecting them be made within a frame of reference embodying particular awareness of the problems of and the problems presented by young people. The challenge to us—one to date only rarely and haphazardly met—is to develop ways of meeting serious juvenile violative behavior that combine considerations of societal protection with concern that the young person will not be further criminalized but will be assisted in growth toward responsible citizenship.

The Functions of the Juvenile Justice System

It can well be argued that the original and still central role of the state—almost its *raison d'etre*—remains the protection of the person and property of the citizens from the depredations of others. A further central necessity is the creation of channels through which the young may grow toward responsible participation in the social order. Various state juvenile court codes since their inception have almost universally included in their statements of purpose clauses something like that of the current Illinois Juvenile Court Act: "The purpose of this Act is to secure for each minor subject hereto such care and guidance as will

serve . . . the welfare of the minor and the best interests of the community" (Article 1, sec. 1–2).

The early framers of the juvenile court appear to have seen little
problem in its stated duality of purpose. They quite comfortably represented that protection of the community was to be by the rehabilitation
of the offender and his reintegration into conforming society. The present state of the "rehabilitative ideal" in juvenile corrections will be
discussed in later chapters. It will suffice to note here the obvious fact of
current pervasive disillusionment with the capacity of the state to intervene therapeutically so successfully as to render unnecessary other
forms of protection against the misdeeds of the lawless young. The
present fashion, therefore, is to dismiss any remaining consideration
that the stance of the juvenile justice system should be in any significant
way rehabilitative as idle daydream of softheaded idealists or as the
stubborn clinging by outmoded professionals to undeserved preferment.

As the concept of the rehabilitative ideal loses credence, alternative
models come to the fore. Essentially, the alternatives are only three in
number, although they may operate in combination: the societal mission and role of the juvenile justice system is variously said to focus
about the exactment of retribution from the offender, the strengthening
of the deterrent power of the law, or the treatment of the offender in
such manner that he is incapacitated from offending again. It thus
becomes necessary to examine the value and knowledge base supporting
these models, and to assess the degree to which they offer a more
feasible framework for social policy than does the one they are to
supplant.

Retribution

The most ancient, most pervasive, and most powerful theme governing
the practice of justice is that of retribution. Retribution is society's endeavor to maintain a connection between the individual's behavior and its
consequences. As the eighteenth-century German philosopher Immanuel
Kant observed in his classic discussion of justice and punishment,

When . . . someone who delights in annoying and vexing peace-
loving folk receives at last a right good beating, it is certainly an

ill, but everyone approves of it and considers it as good in itself even if nothing further results from it; nay, even he who gets the beating must acknowledge, in his reason, that justice has been done to him, because he sees the proportion between welfare and well-doing, which reason inevitably holds before him, here put into practice. (Ezorsky 1972:102)

Further, retribution expresses societal condemnation of violative behavior, supporting the moralizing, norm-upholding function of the law. And on its grimmer side, retribution provides the inevitable outlet for the fear and anger that the offender engenders in the hearts of the citizenry. Unless those deep emotions are kept within legally determined bounds, the passion for revenge may well find darker channels. Criminal law has been likened to the marriage bed in that both provide societally prescribed outlets for inevitable human passions.

Necessary and inevitable though it is, however, retribution is a dissatisfying base on which to build a social purpose and a concomitant societal institution. Criminal justice must uphold the ideal of a relationship between violative behavior and its consequences but can realize the ideal only in the most crudely distorted of forms. It can at best provide only a negative consequence. Further, most offenders are never brought to justice. When they are, only the wildest approximation of a consequence proportionate to their offenses in a measured and understandable way may be achieved. And in contemporary Western societies the passion for revenge is hardly considered one of the loftier human ambitions. Consequently, the appeal to retribution will never be a rallying call for people dedicated to public service in a democratic society. The arm of government dedicated to the performance of a retributive mission can hope for no more than grudging support and for status only as an agent of which citizens are vaguely ashamed. The societal confrontation with the offender will inevitably involve more than retribution. It is the nature of that "more" that is today at issue.

Deterrence

The deterrent function of the criminal justice system has two major aspects. One is concerned with so treating the offender that he will be deterred from further offenses. Conceived of in this way, deterrence is simply one form of individual treatment and must be evaluated as are other interventions calculated to change the behavior of identified offenders. But the aspect of deterrence most commonly considered in connection with social policy is "general deterrence": the publicized imposition of sanctions on detected offenders as a means of discouraging other persons from offenses. There would appear to be little question that one of the functions of the justice system is the maintenance of the deterrent power of the law by retaining a realistic threat of negative consequence from violative behavior.

We are not among those who belittle the efficacy with which this function is accomplished. Indeed, it seems to us that the criminal justice system exercises a powerful effect on most people most of the time. In its absence, we would suffer a great deal more crime than we do at present. The proposition is difficult to test empirically, but Andenaes (1974) and others have noted, for example, that the mass arrest of the Copenhagen police force by the Nazis is 1944 and police strikes in Liverpool in 1919 and in Montreal in 1956 were followed by massive increases in crime.

However, the necessary policy choices do not include the *elimination* of the deterrent threat. Our concern is whether the efficacy of the threat may be altered by marginal manipulations in the certainty or severity of punishment. Unfortunately, neither the necessary empirical knowledge, an adequate theoretical foundation, nor an answer to troubling ethical issues are available as guides to such manipulation. The past fifteen years or so have seen a number of research endeavors to test for variations in deterrence resulting from the imposition of greater or lesser sanctioning certainty or severity. None of these endeavors focuses specifically on juvenile crime. However, the nature of the problem presented to policymakers quickly becomes clear when the studies of deterrent effects in general are examined.

Typically, the studies in question rest upon examination of the degree to which crime rates in selected states or standard metropolitan statistical areas vary with some measure of either the certainty or the severity of sanction. Crime rates are usually measured by Uniform Crime Reports data on index crimes. Certainty of sanction is measured by a variety of statistics, among the more common being the risk of arrest, measured by either the police clearance rate or the conviction rate in the jurisdiction, or the risk of imprisonment, measured by the ratio of prison commitments to reported crimes. Severity of sanction is sometimes measured by mean or median time served in prison. The hypothesis tested is that in the jurisdiction in question, the crime rate will vary negatively with the measure of certainty or severity of sanction; that is, the crime rate will decrease as certainty or severity increases, and vice versa.

Several excellent summaries of these studies exist. The most often quoted and perhaps the most impressive is that of a Panel on Research on Deterrent and Incapacitative Effects appointed by the National Academy of Sciences. The report of this panel focuses on the scientific validity of the pertinent research on the topic (Blumstein, et al. 1978). Numerous other scholars present similar overviews, some reaching more to ethical and social policy issues than did the panel (Zimring and Hawkins 1973; Cook 1980; Andenaes 1966; and others).

With few exceptions, the reports do indicate that crime rates vary negatively to at least some degree with the risk of apprehension, conviction, or imprisonment. Findings on the relationship between crime rates and the lengths of prison terms are equivocal, varying from study to study.

The findings have led to frequent, sometimes vociferous claims that the pathway to crime reduction is through changes in sanctioning policies. Such claims are not clearly justified, in spite of the fact that many of the studies have been painstakingly undertaken and make use of elaborately sophisticated statistical methodology. Unfortunately, they often do not make equally diligent use of readily available knowledge on the fallibility of available data on crime rates or of close awareness of the actual operation of the criminal justice system.

The outcome measure employed in the deterrent studies is almost always the number of crimes reported by police as having occurred in the relevant jurisdiction. But as we noted earlier, it is probable that only some 50 percent of crimes *committed* (as measured, for example, by victim surveys) are ever reported to the police—the figure being higher for some crimes and lower for others. The proportion of crimes reported to police may well vary from time to time and from place to place with variation in general confidence in police or other aspects of police-community relationships, by social class or racial composition of communities, or by police data-gathering or reporting practices. Thus, variations in the number of crimes reported could result from differing levels of fear of sanctions, but could also very well result from differing reporting and recording practices.

Even more damaging to the deterrence studies is the assumption underlying them that correlation demonstrates one-way causal relationships. To anyone with a reasonable degree of awareness of the actual operation of the criminal justice system, that supposition simply seems naive. In actuality, variation in apprehension, conviction, or sentencing rates may often be a result rather than a cause of variation in crime rates. Increased tolerance of criminality, with resultant less frequent recourse to sanctions, may exist or develop in jurisdictions in which crime is more common. A system overload may result in wearied police becoming more selective in arresting, in prosecuting attorneys more frequently accepting plea bargains for reduced charges, and in judges avoiding commitment to overcrowded institutions. Offenses that seem shocking in low-crime jurisdictions and there resulting in severe sanctions may come to seem "more of the same" to the more blasé judge in a high-crime, central city area, and may result in much less severe sanctions. It is also conceivable that areas with relatively low crime rates provide police with greater opportunity to pursue and detect offenders for whom conviction and sentencing are likely. Such speculation is difficult to test empirically. However, an interesting exploratory study by Pontell (1978) does adduce data supportive of a hypothesis that variation in crime rates tends to be prior to and inversely correlated with variation in certainty of punishment.

Seeking to overcome these problems, some studies have adopted a quasi-experimental or even, in a few instances, experimental approach to the examination of the deterrent effects of different sanction measures. These studies are excellently reviewed and summarized in the volume reporting the findings of the National Academy of Sciences Panel (Blumstein et al. 1978:53–59; Nagin 1978:95-139; Zimring 1981:140–86). They include such experiments as those with preventive police patrol in Kansas City, aggressive police field interrogation in San Diego (stopping, questioning, and sometimes frisking subjects who have aroused police officers' suspicions), and differing strategies for coping with income tax evasion. Quasi-experiments have endeavored to examine the effects of sudden changes in laws governing sanctions or in practices regarding the application of sanctions. These have included the introduction of special patrols in New York subways, increasing the number of police in a high-crime precinct in New York City, enactment of motorcyclist helmet laws, aggressive police action and/or imposition of severe sanctions for drunken driving in Chicago, Britain, and Scandinavia, the effect of lowering the legal drinking age on fatal motor crashes, and the decriminalization of abortion in Hawaii (Frances Gallagher cited in Blumstein, et al. 1978:174–86).

Of these studies we must regretfully agree with the National Academy of Sciences Panel's conclusion:

> The results of experimental and quasi-experimental studies of deterrence are mixed, with some finding evidence of significant deterrent effects and others finding no evidence of change in crime rates. In most cases, however, the research designs suffer from a variety of flaws, many of which are remediable, that undermine confidence in the results. All too often, other factors can be identified to explain positive or negative findings, and thus the analyses fail to provide any valid evidence on deterrent effects. (Blumstein et al. 1978:54–55)

All this is not to say that we believe sanctions to be useless. They must exist, and it is quite probable that in some instances increased sanctions may deter some crime. But we remain almost completely ignorant of the answers to questions as to *which* sanctions, increased *how much*, will reduce *what sorts* of crime, by *what amounts*, at *what costs* in terms of dollars, overloaded criminal justice agencies, threats to civil liberties, or criminalization of offenders previously less exposed to the ministrations of such systems. Arguments for changes in sanctioning policy based on the presumed availability of empirical evidence of effectiveness are quite simply not warranted.

The problem of generating and drawing conclusions from research-based data on the deterrent effect is enormously aggravated by the current absence of any coherent body of theory on punishment and crime. Knowledge that human beings will at least tend to behave so as to avoid painful consequences does not provide an adequate basis for social policy. Quite obviously, various behaviors are differentially attractive to different persons and thus constitute widely differing behavioral compulsions. By the same token, consequences fearful to some are not particularly so to others. One can hardly imagine the formulation of a body of theory that will bring into a useful whole the reaction to legal threat of the middle-class businessman, the frustrated and hopeless underclass minority knowing nothing but a life of idleness interrupted by brief periods of marginal employment, the "hit man" for the rackets, the compulsion-driven sex offender, and the character disorder that prevents its possessor from even foreseeing the relationship between his behavior and its consequences.

The problem is probably particularly acute as it bears upon the violative behaviors of children and youths. As we have previously noted, the assumption that youthful violative behavior is consistently—or even frequently—a product of careful, rational weighing of future consequences against present gratification may not be justified. Even more frustrating to the proponents of deterrence policy is the fact that it may be dauntingly difficult to actually increase the degree to which juvenile illegal behavior does result in sanctions. At present, although reliable data are nonexistent, estimates of the probability of offenses by juveniles leading to the imposition of sanctions would generally be in the same ball park as that suggested by Nejelski (1976:95): "of every 500 possible juvenile arrests, it is estimated that there are 200 police contacts, resulting in 100 arrests. Of these, only 40 youths are taken in, only 20 appear before a judge, and only 2 or 3 are sent to a correctional institution." Even so, many juvenile institutions are filled to capacity and appear to have exhausted legislative willingness to allocate new funds.

Let us suppose, nonetheless, that a situation could be achieved in which double the present proportion of offenses resulted in institutional sanction. Would a 4 to 6 percent, instead of a 2 to 3 percent probability of incarceration even be evident to the target population? Would not rational calculation—if it can be expected—still indicate a quite acceptably low level of risk from tempting violative behavior, particularly to the youngster in the neighborhoods in which delinquency seems most rampant, neighborhoods in which legitimate ladders to gratification are often nonexistent and in which little disgrace may be attached to having spent a brief spell in a juvenile institution?

Out of the jumble of uncertainties about manipulating deterrents arise a series of troubling ethical issues. Under what circumstances is a democratic society justified in using the welfare of an individual as a means, rather than as an end, and thus imposing suffering upon him as a means of influencing others? What degree of loss of freedom is justified as a means of deterrence when the resultant extent of deterrence, if it exists at all, is unknown? The answers to such questions may be little troubling in an authoritarian state. In a state grounded in belief in the primacy of human freedom and the worth of the individual, the same questions become unanswerable. Deterrence alone becomes an unacceptable basis for social policy governing the encounter between the state and the offender.

Incapacitation

The oft-repeated plea that the juvenile justice system protect the community by "getting off the streets" the dangerous juvenile offender surely has some justification. Few would deny society's right—even obligation—to deprive of their freedom those who would persistently deny to others the security of property and person. Theoretically, then, it should be possible for the state to increase considerably the citizen's protection from the repeat offender. Further, it should be possible to assess in advance the degree to which increased protection would result from increasing the rate at which identified offenders are sentenced to custodial care or subjected to lengthier sentences. One should simply calculate the rate at which the average offender had been offending prior to his apprehension (the number of his offenses per year, for example) and multiply this by the number of years served. The result should constitute the number of offenses avoided by incapacitation.

Calculations of this sort are sometimes attempted, usually focusing on adults but occasionally on juveniles. (For a review of such studies, their findings, and their problems, see Cohen 1978). Unfortunately, the findings to date do not provide a very helpful basis for the formulation of social policy. As Cohen (1978:230) notes, "there is general agreement that the incapacitative effect of current CJS [Criminal Justice System] policies is not very large. The crimes averted do not account for a very significant portion of the crimes committed." Further, there is disagreement among the authors of the available studies concerning the potential gains in incapacitation if prison use were expanded.

Those studies focusing on the incapacitation of juveniles, in particular, tend either to suggest no firm conclusions or to cast grave doubts on the feasibility of increased use of incarceration as a means of reducing juvenile crime. It is quite true that the available evidence indicates that chronic offenders are responsible for a quite disproportionate share of juvenile offense behavior. Unfortunately, the evidence also indicates that the numbers of chronic offenders considerably exceed the capacities of our society to control them through incarceration. Among the best illustrations of this fact is the analysis provided by Hamparian et al. (1978:7) of the picture developed by Wolfgang et al. (1972) from their justifiably famous study of the arrest careers of a cohort composed of males born in Philadelphia in 1945 and continuing to reside there between the ages of 10 and 18—a total of 9,945 youths. Of the 10,214 known offenses committed by these youths, 51.9 percent were attributable to a relatively small group of 627 chronic offenders comprising 18 percent of the total of those ever delinquent or 6 percent of the total cohort. Nonwhites were over four and one-half times more likely to fall in the chronic offender group than were whites: 14.4 percent versus 3.0 percent of the total group divided by race (Wolfgang et al. 1972:88–90). Wolfgang suggests, "It is clear that . . . any social action that could stop these delinquent cases before they go beyond their fourth delinquency would decrease significantly the number of offenses committed by a birth cohort. Such social action, if concentrated on the lower SES chronic offenders, would not only reduce the amount but also the seriousness of the offenses committed" (ibid.:105).

Hamparian and her associates bring Wolfgang's suggestion to its obvious conclusion. Taking into consideration the fact that the age period presenting the highest risk of criminal offending is 14–24 and that the incapacitation recommended by Wolfgang et al. would thus need to run until the upper part of that range, they note that

The reader is left to muse over the implications of the only known social intervention certain to stop a delinquent in any point in his career: incarceration. Turning to the *Statistical Abstract of the United States,* we find that in 1975 there were 22,803,000 males between the ages of 14 and 24 in the United States. This figure is divided between 19,490,000 whites and 3,312,000 blacks. If we apply the percentages of each race in the Philadelphia cohort that Wolfgang found to be chronic offenders—14.4 percent of the blacks and 3.0 percent of the whites—to these totals, we arrive at a figure of 1,062,000 potential chronic offenders in the 14 to 24 age zone. Undoubtedly, the figure is too high. Crime rates in Philadelphia are relatively high, certainly higher than in rural and small town America, and the percentage of potential chronics in the national population is surely lower. Perhaps the true figure would be in the 500,000 to 750,000 range. But even at that, these potential chronics would exceed by far the 47,000 juveniles held in correctional facilities of all kinds throughout the nation in 1975. (Hamparian et al. 1978:7)

The reader might muse a bit further, of course, on the probable reaction of the public of any large city to the announcement of a social policy calling for the incarceration of 14.4 percent of that city's black youths and 3 percent of its white youths. And such musings might be further titillated by consideration of the fact that much of the delinquency averted by locking up so large a portion of the city's population would be of a minor nature. Thus Monahan (1981:72) summarizes the portion of Wolfgang's research carrying his Philadelphia cohort up to age 30. The 6 percent of the cohort classed as chronic offenders (having experienced 5 arrests) by age 18 had grown to 15 percent by age 30. The probability of a fifth arrest (for any crime) given four "priors" was 0.80. But the probability of a fifth *serious* ("index" offense) arrest was 0.36. Even with 10 previous arrests, the probability of an eleventh arrest for a serious offense was 0.42. The majority of those youths who had experienced five prior arrests and thus would have been "incapacitated" under a policy calling for incarceration after such a record would not have been arrested for a subsequent serious offense if not incarcerated.

The possible advantages of greatly increased use of incapacitation are rendered even more dubious if the possibility is considered that incarceration may result in the production of more frequent and more serious offenders. Again, the data permit only speculation. But Wolfgang et al. note from their study of their Philadelphia cohort that, while the effect of disposition on subsequent offense histories is unclear,

It appears that the juvenile justice system has been able to isolate the hard core offenders fairly well. Unfortunately, the product of this encounter with sanctioning authorities is far from desirable. Not only do a greater number of those who receive punitive treatment (institutionalization, fine, or probation) continue to violate the law, but they also commit more serious crimes with greater rapidity than those who experience a less constraining contact with the judicial and correctional systems. (Wolfgang et al. 1972:252)

Hamparian et al (1978), in the study of their cohort of violent juvenile offenders in Columbus, Ohio, note patterns tending to confirm those presented by Wolfgang. They studied time intervals between offenses "controlling for such variables as arrest sequence number, types of offense, age, race, sex, and socioeconomic status." They report that "Perhaps the most significant finding in this study is that with all else controlled, there is a moderate to high inverse relationship between the severity of the sanction for the first in every pair of crimes and the arrest for the second in every pair . . . incarceration *reduced* the net months to next arrest by 4.81 months, jail detention by 1.23 months, and formal supervision by 0.80. Only the least intrusive alternatives, grouped together here under the heading of informal supervision, increased street time. The figure was 2.71 months" (Hamparian et al. 1978:119; emphasis in original.)

Petersilia (1980) summarizes the findings of three cohort studies of persons of both sexes born in Racine, Wisconsin, in 1942, 1949, and 1955 and totaling over six thousand members. In each cohort, males tended toward greater involvement with the police after age 18 as the number of contacts and the seriousness of the sanctions before age 18 increased (p. 367).

There are, of course, two possible sorts of explanation for the rather startling data presented by the cohort studies. First, it may be supposed that the juvenile justice systems studied did succeed in identifying a group of youngsters with offense propensities so high that they were very likely to offend again, and offend with increased rapidity, no matter what treatment they were accorded. In such cases, one can only conclude that the justice systems concerned were ineffective in their endeavors to protect the public through incapacitation. But the second, even more alarming possibility must be considered: it may be that coercive intervention tends to be criminogenic and that incarceration, in particular, tends to produce more frequent subsequent offenders.

Neither explanation is certain. But both are discouraging. It seems to us that the one line of exploration does not preclude the other, and that both probably contribute to a disappointing result.

Against the somewhat dubious benefit of turning to increased use of incapacitation as a delinquency control policy must be set its costs. The present is a time of almost desperate financial straits for most state governments. Tax incomes are falling as the demand for social services of all kinds increases. Most states' juvenile correctional institutions' capacities are exhausted. Youths are being hurriedly rushed out the back door in order to admit others at the front. Overcrowding brings lowered morale on the part of both staff and inmates, increased depersonalization of care, and, too often, increased brutalization. The financial burden is enormous. An annual, per-bed operating cost of $20,000 to $40,000 is not at all unusual. New construction may be expected to cost $40,000 to $80,000 per single-bed unit. Few state legislatures are likely in the immediate future to allocate funds to increase present resources to such degree as to make feasible any marked increase in capacity.

As least in theory, the problem could be eased if methodologies could be developed whereby we could predict with reasonable certainty *which* offenders would seriously offend again, incapacitate them, and return those not predicted to be serious recidivists to the community. Unfortunately, it has not yet been demonstrated that such prediction is possible. We have noted above that in the major large-scale study of juvenile offense records available (the Philadelphia cohort study) a history of as many as ten arrests produced a probability of only 0.42 of a future arrest for an index-type offense. But what, then, of the possibility of turning to the professional judgments of clinicians to increase our predictive capacity? The available evidence is not finally conclusive, but it is discouraging.

The Prediction of Dangerousness

Recent major studies of the abilities of mental health professionals to predict law-violative behavior have most usually been of efforts to predict violence on the part of adults. They have been helpfully summarized by Monahan (1981:72–80). For example, Kozol et al. (1972)

report a study of 592 male offenders examined at the Massachusetts Center for the Diagnosis and Treatment of Dangerous Persons. Most subjects had histories of dangerous crimes. Each offender was examined independently by at least two psychiatrists, two psychologists, and a social worker, aided by a battery of psychological tests and a "meticulous reconstruction of the life history." Checks on predictions after five years revealed that only 8 percent of those diagnosed as not dangerous were known to have committed a serious assaultive act, while 34.7 percent of those diagnosed as dangerous were known to have committed such an act. The practitioners' predictions obviously did have some validity. Yet, 65 percent of these previous offenders, diagnosed after exhaustive study as being dangerous, were not known to have committed a dangerous act. Predictions were wrong in two out of three cases, as far as could be determined.

Other, somewhat similar studies of the results of clinical predictions of dangerousness include two studies of patients released from Maryland's Patuxent Institution, one study of patients released in New York state as a result of a Supreme Court holding that Johnnie Baxstrom had been denied equal protection of the law by being held beyond his maximum sentence in an institution for the criminally insane on grounds that he continued to be "dangerous" (*Baxstrom v. Herold*, 1966), and one of a somewhat similar group of "mentally disordered offenders" in Pennsylvania. In these four studies, the proportions of offenders diagnosed as "dangerous" and liable to commit further violent acts actually revealed by follow-up studies to have committed such acts were 41.3, 20.0, 14.0, and 14.0, respectively. The 41.3 percent success rate was achieved in one of the two Patuxent studies and resulted from including in the successful prediction group all known offenses, rather than only those of violence, as in the other studies.

A variety of attempts have been made to improve upon the accuracy of clinical prediction by the use of actuarial tables employing determined statistical relationships between identified variables and recidivism. Again, the focus has usually been on violence. Thus, Wenk et al. (1972) report a California Youth Authority study of 4,146 wards in which psychiatric diagnoses and psychological battery tests were employed. Subjects were followed for 15 months after their parole from Youth Authority institutions, and data on 100 variables were analyzed to determine which were predictive of recidivism. *No combination of* *variables attained a better than 8 to 1 false positive to true positive ratio in predicting reconviction and return to prison on violence charges.**

True, an occasional study reports somewhat more impressive results. Thus, Monahan (1981:102–4) describes a Michigan Department of Corrections project employing actuarial tables referring to nature of past offense, institutional adjustment, and age of first arrest to predict arrests for violent offense of prison parolees. About 5 percent of the study population was identified as being "very high risk." In a mean follow-up period of 14 months, 40 percent recidivated, as measured by arrests for violent crimes. Certainly, considerable predictive powers had been achieved, but, even so, six out of every ten parolees identified as "very high risk" are not known to have again committed violent offenses.

There are, of course, flaws in the available research data that limit their usefulness as predictors of future violative behavior on the part of juveniles. The most obvious potential for error arises from the fact that is has been possible to test the accuracy of predictions only against *recorded arrest.* It may be that much violent violative behavior does not lead to arrest. However, Monahan (1981:82–86) rather persuasively argues that actual predictive accuracy may approximate that shown by the studies. National surveys of samples of the population indicate that only 47 percent of the people who said they had been victims of violent crimes had reported such crimes to the police (U.S. Department of Justice 1978). Such reports to police lead to arrest in about 50 percent of the cases (FBI 1978). From these data, we might conclude that most offenders predicted to recidivate actually do so but are not apprehended. It is also true that various studies show that recidivists arrested for injury offenses, when interviewed in research projects, report that they had actually committed 7 to 10 felonies per arrest. Thus the one-third or so individuals predicted to recidivate and actually arrested may well have committed most of the unsolved crimes. It may well be that

---

*The problem of false positives is dramatically illustrated by a hypothetical example from Livermore et al. (1968), quoted in Rutter and Giller (1984:285): "Assume that one person out of a thousand will kill. Assume also that an exceptionally accurate test is created which differentiates with 95 percent effectiveness those who will kill from those who will not. If 100,000 people were tested, out of the 100 who would kill, 95 would be isolated. Unfortunately, out of the 99,900 who would not kill, 4,995 people would also be isolated as potential killers. In these circumstances, it is clear that we could not justify isolating all 5,090 people."

the proportion of "false positive" predictions revealed in the prediction studies provides a reasonably accurate estimate of the persons predicted to violently recidivate but not having done so. It may well be true that some two-thirds of those predicted to again commit crimes of violence will not actually do so. If predictive accuracy were the only goal, much better results could be achieved by simply predicting that no one would recidivate!

There are, of course, further considerations necessitating caution in generalizing too widely from the available studies of predictive accuracy. Most studies have been of adult populations, in confinement, and the behavior predicted has been violence. Predictions have covered long time spans—several months or even years. Failure to predict events in so distant a future must not be taken as demonstrating inability to predict more adequately the immediate future, as may be desirable, for example, in considering release from temporary detention pending court hearing. But consideration of final disposition of serious delinquency cases would appear to present difficulties at least as great as those involved in the prediction studies. The data strongly suggest that in order to avoid recidivist behavior on the part of one offender through incarceration, we must be prepared to incarcerate two or three who would not recidivate if returned to the community. The fundamental issues are those of values; how many persons are we willing to hold in institutions in order to incapacitate one who would offend? In view of the present—and apparently eternal—overcrowded and overstressed condition of the criminal and juvenile justice agencies, how much greater a share of the available tax dollar should be allocated to incapacitation rather than to other societal concerns?

No formulas exist for answering these questions. The necessity for delicate and difficult human judgment cannot be evaded, and the thrusting of this fact to the forefront of the current discourse is the constant duty of the social policy analyst.

It is worth noting that the problem of predicting dangerousness among juvenile and adult offenders does not merely reflect the lack of a sophisticated methodology that has been achieved elsewhere in the social sciences. The undeniable truth is that predictions in the social sciences generally have a notoriously poor track record, and that substantial gains in accuracy seem unlikely. Our inability to predict delinquency and crime seems little different from our frustrated efforts to predict reliably rates of inflation, demographic trends, group behavior, and countless other social phenomena. As Alasdair MacIntyre noted in his *After Virtue* (1981:85): "For the central function of the social scientist as expert advisor or manager is to predict the outcomes of alternative policies, and if his predictions do not derive from a knowledge of law-like generalisations, the status of social scientist as predictor becomes endangered—as, so it turns out, it ought to be; for the record of social scientists as predictors is very bad indeed, insofar as the record can be pieced together."

In summary, then, retribution, deterrence, and incapacitation are all inevitable goals in the confrontation between society and the juvenile offender. But none of them—particularly when considered alone—is wholly satisfying intellectually or ethically. None answers the question of what to do about the juvenile delinquent. When carefully examined, the proposals of the hard liner contain elements of unsupported wishful thinking that are quite as pervasive as those underlying the supposedly soft approaches that the hard liner so scorns. Further, when operation- alized each proposal carries with it latent consequences dangerous to the goals of a society oriented to the worth of the individual human. We are reminded of a brief comment on the personal philosophy of Charles Dickens, the source of which we have been unable to discover, but which we consider to be nonetheless apt. Dickens' eloquence sprang in part from his own early deprivation, including horrified humiliation at his father's incarceration in debtors' prison. It is noted that "He [Dick- ens] regarded violence as the necessary end of violence; prison as the consequence of prison; hatred as the wages of hatred."

We turn, then, to an examination of whether something might be retrieved from the rehabilitationist as well as the hard liner approach and to determine whether a useful synthesis employing the positive element of each position might be possible.

Return to the Rehabilitative Ideal?

As we have previously noted, the position of the rehabilitationist differs from that of the hard liner in most dimensions, beginning with its fundamental view of human nature and the origins of behavior. Humanity is seen as of very broad potential, with personality, motivations, and behavior all resulting from the interaction between genetic endowment and lifelong environmental experience. Thus it is incorrect to perceive the offender as one who has surveyed wide ranges of behavioral opportunities and rationally chosen among them. Instead, his range of choice may be very narrow indeed, and his behavior may best be perceived as influenced to a considerable degree by his past experience and present situation. The task becomes one of understanding and intervening in such a way as to enable the individual to function as a conforming member of society, having the desire and the opportunity to do so.

The rehabilitationist's emphasis is upon compassion, upon the essential worth of the individual, and upon the responsibility of the democratic society to ensure the availability of pathways to the fulfillment of human potential, along with frank recognition of the community's right to protection. The goals are lofty, and they have led to a lofty rhetoric. The central issues, however, have to do with the substance behind the rhetoric and with the actual achievability of the ideal of rehabilitation.

Among the problems encountered in conceptualizing the rehabilitationist approach, largely based as it is upon a philosophy of determinism, is the fact that there has emerged as yet no coherent, generally accepted, and empirically demonstrated body of theory specifying the nature of the causal factors "determining" violative behavior. This is in spite of the fact that several generations of dedicated and capable scholars have devoted much of their careers to the study of the "etiology of delinquency." A variety of approaches have been followed, several leading to dazzling theoretical pyramids, richly complex, sophisticatedly elaborated, and intuitively appealing. These accomplishments clearly do shed light upon a variety of aspects of the problem. But each operates upon a different set of assumptions, usually untested or untestable. Each focuses upon different aspects of reality, with the connections between them yet to be established. This confusing situation is best illustrated by a brief review of currently dominant approaches.

Various though they are, the current approaches to the explanation of violative behavior tend to cluster in two major groupings. The first, which tends to dominate most actual work with offenders, focuses on the personality of the offender and on the origins of his proclivities toward conventional or violative behavior. The target of help and for change is thus the individual offender and his patterns of coping with the external world. The second grouping of causal theories is concerned largely with environmental forces associated with community, subculture, and culture-group living. These forces are seen as both defining behavioral expectations and determining the opportunities for and limitations upon social functioning. Thus the target for intervention is the complex of social, cultural, economic, and environmental forces seen as leading to particular ways of life.

Personality Theory

During the first half of the twentieth century, the most widely accepted explanations of the "roots of crime" tended to be those based on personality theory and advanced by psychiatrists, psychologists, and social workers. One could—and many of us did—conjure works such as those of Alexander and Staub (1956), Healy and Bronner (1936), August Aichorn (1935), Kate Friedlander (1947), Jenkins and Hewitt (1944), Redl and Wineman (1951), and many others. In general, they focused on the psychic life and the personality of the individual delinquent, conceived as emerging largely from genetic endowment shaped by intimate associations with other persons, beginning in infancy. Humans were seen as inheriting a core of instinctual drives and needs for wish fulfillment. Growing up as social beings demands learning to adapt these drives and needs so as to gain satisfaction in a world in which dependence on others is universal. However, faulty experience during the growth years may result in the child's failure to move toward mature, flexible relationships with others upon whom gratification of needs depends. Such failure may lead, in turn, to retention of the "I want what I want when I want it" patterns of infancy. Or, at the other extreme, an overrigid environment may lead to the suppression of powerful needs so that they exist only unconsciously and find expression in explosive or disguised forms. In either event, violative behavior may result, often from origins of which the subject is not consciously aware.

While a wide variety of forms of this very briefly sketched theoretical framework have undergirded the efforts of several generations of practitioners, its most systematic and large-scale operationalization has probably resulted from the development by the California Youth Authority (the state's juvenile correctional agency) of its famous Inter-Personal

Maturity Level (I-level) classification system. In this structure, personality development is conceived as taking place through successive stages of integration of perception of self and the environment.

Under the I-level system, delinquents are classed into three of five basic maturity levels and then into subtypes within each such level. The nine resulting classifications are:

Maturity Level 2. Individuals whose interpersonal understanding and behavior reflect their demands that the world should take care of them. Other persons are seen as "givers" or "withholders."

(1) Asocial, aggressive. Responds with active demand and open hostility when frustrated.

(2) Asocial, passive. Responds with whining, complaining, and withdrawal when frustrated.

Maturity Level 3. Sees interpersonal world in only crudely differentiated terms and with only beginning understanding of how one's own behavior influences behavior of others toward him. Unable to achieve in a long-range sense or to plan for the future.

(3) Immature conformist. Responds with immediate compliance to whomever seems to have power at the moment.

(4) Cultural conformist. Responds with conformity to specific reference group, delinquent peers.

(5) Manipulator. Operates so as to undermine and usurp power of others.

Maturity Level 4. Has internalized set of standards by which own behavior and that of others is judged and has some ability to relate to people emotionally. Is concerned about status and respect and is influenced by people he admires.

(6) Neurotic, acting out. Responds to underlying guilt by overt behavior.

(7) Neurotic, anxious. Responds with symptoms of emotional disturbance to conflict produced by feelings of inadequacy and guilt.

(8) Situational emotional reaction. Acts out in response to immediate personal or familial crisis.

(9) Cultural identifier. Responds to identification with a deviant value system by living out his delinquent beliefs. (California Department of the Youth Authority n.d.:3–5)

The maturing personality grows toward understanding of the self, of one's impact upon others, and of the relationship between others' needs and one's own. Should the individual become fixated in one of the early stages of development, he is likely to meet his needs in a socially inappropriate or deviant way. Lacking effective internalized behavioral standards and unable to assess the reactions of others to his own behavior, he takes what he wants without regard for others and their rights. Or, at the other end of the scale, the "neurotic" develops internalized standards that are overly rigid or otherwise inappropriate.

The I-level framework has provided a theoretical base for programs responsible for thousands of delinquent youths in California. These have stimulated similar programs in many other states, in Canada, and in Europe. They represent the major attempt to date to develop typologies of delinquent youths and to relate them to differential treatment needs. Thus, for example, some data seem to suggest that youths tending toward the neurotic pole are most likely to make successful community adjustments if returned directly to community living, while certain types of less interpersonally mature "power oriented" serious delinquents (a group combining the "cultural conformists" and "manipulators" described above) do best if first subjected to a period of institutional care as a means of confrontation with reality (Palmer 1974). In juvenile probation, the I-level system seems to have demonstrated the desirability of matching offender types to workers' personalities and styles (Barkwell 1980).

Other etiological theories focusing on delinquents as individuals are concerned largely with possible biological, usually inherited, causal factors. According to this approach, for example, the emotionally shallow "psychopath," unable to control impulses or to learn from punishment, experiencing little remorse or guilt, and incapable of depth in interpersonal relationships may suffer from genetic neurological abnormalities. Such abnormalities may be revealed in electronically measurable variations from norms in neural functioning (Mednick and Volavka 1980). It must be noted, however, that present understandings of such abnormalities and of their impact upon personality and behavior are limited indeed, and provide little or no basis for the formulation of social policy. Psychobiological research was long shunned in the United States as being somehow antiegalitarian. But the research has experienced at least a degree of resurgence in recent years, and the future *may* bring clearer perception of biological as well as social and cultural influences *and of their interactions* in the etiology of behavior.

Sociocultural Theory

Much relevant and instructive theory focuses not so much—or at all—on the complexities of the individual's proclivities as it does upon variations in behavior patterns arising from social class, ethnic group, subculture, or broader cultural membership. Such groupings are seen as defining for their members the nature of expected behavior and as determining the social, political, and economic opportunities and limitations upon that behavior. Much of the thinking harks back to the "differential association" format propounded before World War II by Edwin Sutherland.

Sutherland (1972) proposed what he believed to be a "universal and sufficient" theory of delinquency, such that violative behavior, as all other behavior, should be considered learned behavior resulting from the degree to which the individual has been exposed to persons defining conventional standards negatively instead of positively. The influence of these definitions was said to vary with the recency, frequency, and intensity of relationships with other persons: family, friends, culture group, and others. The individual delinquent or nondelinquent could thus almost be perceived as the sum of his interpersonal relationships.

To differential association theory scholars such as Shaw (1929), Shaw and McKay ([1942] 1969) and their followers added theories of the origins of values and customs of slum youths. They depicted development of slum subcultures as resulting from the relative isolation of recent immigrants and other deprived groups in the depressed big city areas where most crime, poverty, disease, and other pathologies were to be found. The resultant "delinquent subcultures" were seen as shared and transmitted in the same way and just as compellingly as subcultures in middle-class areas. Glaser (1979:207) aptly sums up this school of thought when he notes that Shaw and McKay conveyed the impression that "it is as normal for a slum boy to become delinquent as it is for a Parisian boy to learn French."

More recent sociological theory tends to depict subcultural variations in values, beliefs, and behavior as being delimited by and very often expressive of the pervasive U.S. middle-class culture. That culture is seen as imposing its standards, values, and goals upon all subcultures. In particular, all American youths are inculcated with the dominant importance placed upon material success. They learn to define their own worth and that of others by the degree to which success is achieved. The "American myth" further teaches that failure in the struggle for successful achievement in this "land of opportunity" is a matter of personal fault. However, the harsh reality is that lower-class youths are born into situations in which prevailing ways of behaving, numbers of available "contacts" necessary to success, other opportunities for education or employment, and absence of positive adult role models all mitigate against success as defined by middle-class standards. Such youths find themselves in the bitter position of having imposed upon them middle-class goals but having nowhere available to them the pathways to achieve those goals. Either as direct means of achieving middle-class goals (Cloward and Ohlin 1960) or as reactions against the broader culture that seems to have no place for them (Cohen 1955), they form their own subcultural groupings, often in the form of delinquent gangs devoted to illegitimate means of achieving the material success and the sense of self-worth necessary to all.

Hirschi (1969) also emphasizes the dominant, broader culture, stressing the manner in which essentially selfish gratification needs common to all are kept under control by bonds with conventional society, attachment to conventional persons, conventional pursuits (employment, civic life, etc.) that would be endangered by delinquent acts, and personal anticriminal beliefs. But some persons in some cultures have their major bonds with offenders and have little opportunity to develop ties to the conventional world. Thus they are not successfully controlled by the standards of that world.

Yet another variation of environmental theory derives from the recent years' writings of economists concerned with the study of crime. They have tended to see humans as highly rational calculators, making inevitable choices dictated by prospects of rewards (largely economic), risks of apprehension, and costs in terms of punishment or loss of opportunity for conventional employment. Thus these scholars have focused on the development of measures of risk of apprehension and severity of resultant cost (punishment). From these measures they endeavor, with thus far varying degrees of success, to predict offense rates.

Finally, earlier we discussed "labeling theory" and the manner in which it depicts deviance as the almost inevitable result of the justice system—the apprehension, separating from conventional groups, and negative labeling of those identified as offenders.

Causation Theory and Intervention Practice

The decades-long efforts on the part of scholars to arrive at understandings of the roots of delinquency and crime have been somewhat fruitful. From them, the practitioner may gain perceptions in depth on the nature of the struggles undergone by those with whom he or she works. Those concerned with social policy may be helped to perceive the complexities and needs of programs calculated to serve offenders and the nature of the societal problems leading to violative behavior. These positives being admitted, however, it must also be admitted that causation theory, in its present state, can at best provide vague and conflicting guidance to practice.

As was, we hope, made clear in the preceding paragraphs, the practitioner or policymaker who hopes to cope with delinquency through alleviating its "root causes" will find wide—and frequently quite hostile—disagreement among learned professionals as to what those causes are. From various schools of thought come exciting gleams of light on facets of the whole. Available to us are rich insights into personality patterns seeming common to many delinquents, into biological differences appearing to be associated with deviant behavior, into the manner in which differing cultural systems contribute to violative or nonviolative behavior, or into the differing opportunity structures available to youths born into various social classes. Each major school probably has some factual ground. But thus far lacking is delinquency theory that brings the discrete facets of truth into an interrelated and coherent whole. Our perception of delinquency disquietingly resembles the blind men's of the elephant, each approaching a different part of the beast.

While seldom essayed or even given explicit recognition, the task of establishing connections among current theoretical perspectives has not wholly been ignored. Daniel Glaser, for example, proposes an approach that he terms "differential anticipation theory" and summarizes as follows:

> a person refrains from or commits a crime because of his or her anticipation of consequences, but anticipations are determined by (i) the person's total conventional and criminal social bonds; (ii) the person's prior social learning experiences that have provided skills, tastes and ideas conducive to gratification in criminal or in

alternative pursuits; and (iii) the person's perceptions of needs, opportunities and risks when interpreting momentary circumstances. (Glaser 1979:217–18)

This and similar attempts to bring order out of a jumble of approaches to causation are helpful in clarifying elements of the problem. But they also highlight the difficulties. Glaser lists three sets of variables at a very high level of abstraction. Many scholars would not be sure that elements important to them are subsumed under Glaser's categories, nor would it seem evident which variables should be considered prior in influence, or how the various elements might be considered in interaction.

In sum, then, a "general field theory" of delinquency (to borrow Einstein's famous phrase) remains a goal for an uncertain future. For the present, it must suffice to acknowledge that human behavior presently appears to result from infinite permutations of possible "causal" factors, some very evident, some so subtle as to be not only unmeasurable but, indeed almost imperceptible from any external position. Broad tendencies toward correlation between certain defined behaviors and other personality or environmental variables may be discerned, but the identification of invariate, direct, and predictable cause-effect relationships permitting even reasonably precise prediction is beyond our present or our foreseeable capacities.

The Bridge to Practice Theory

It may be argued, of course, that while causation research has not identified patterns permitting prediction of behavior in any but probabilistic terms, factors often associated with and apparently at least contributing to violative behavior can be seen. Students of causation theory thus often maintain that criminal justice practice and social policy should be guided by available theory and empirical evidence concerning these apparently contributory causes of crime. Failure to accept such guidance is often—frequently quite bitingly—criticized as resulting in atheoretical practice and policy, without coherent basis or substance, and emerging only as a consequence of a policy vacuum.

Causation theorists' criticisms of current practice and policy are often all too true. But there remains considerable reason to doubt that, even if wholly accepted, present theory would provide an adequate basis for practice and policy. In our opinion, it is too seldom recognized that causation theory is usually far from being practice theory. It may be generally helpful to identify contributory causes—but the task of developing theory, strategies, and tactics enabling us to successfully intervene in causal patterns remains. Causation theory has not, in the main, been developed by practitioners, interested in and aware of practice issues, but by scholars whose most intimate province is much more abstract. It thus provides goals for interventive endeavor at a very high level of abstraction. The necessary next step is the development of the theoretical path and the practice knowledge necessary to the reasoned pursuit of such goals. All too frequently, the gaps remaining until this step is taken are not envisioned.

Intervention as Futility

The policy development problem flows from inherent difficulties even more damaging than the fact that available delinquency-causation theory is not yet fully developed and is subject to wide disagreement. Unfortunately, preoccupation with the enticing call to achieve understanding of ultimate causes frequently leads to misconceptions of the nature of the task of societal intervention into the course of violative behavior. This task then tends to be depicted as hopeless. The obvious conclusion becomes that efforts directed toward rehabilitation, resocialization, prevention, or, indeed, any positive intervention are futile.

Geoffrey Hazard persuasively argues the "intervention is a futile dream" approach today so widely accepted and so limiting efforts at positive intervention:

Perhaps we should begin by recognizing that most of the deviance that the law seeks to control is simply inaccessible from any external position. To the extent that it is caused by psychological factors in the individual, we now know that those factors are hard to identify and harder to modify through legal and governmental processes. To the extent it is cause by the actor's immediate social environment (family, peers, neighborhood), we now know such environments are largely impervious to the intervention of planners. To the extent it is caused by the breakdown of self-control, we now know that inculcating self-control through legal compulsion is essentially a contradiction in terms. To the extent it is caused by chance opportunity, we now know that the state cannot establish controls on the exigencies of everyday life. (Hazard 1976:18)

Hazard's and similar statements are probably accurate reflections of the difficulty of eliminating root causes of delinquency. But they may be quite wrong in their conclusion that therefore positive societal intervention in the course of delinquency is impossible. Such conclusions would seem to arise from a faulty perception of the nature of "cause" in human affairs. The "causes" of deviant behavior thus far identified do not constitute an implacable fate irresistibly compelling a narrowly defined end. The broad factors noted by Hazard are best understood as contributory or contingent causes, producing a specific consequence only in favorable constellation with little understood arrays of other imponderables, some arising from within and some from without the personality. Most youths suffering psychological problems, immersed in unfavorable social environments, evincing less than the usual capacity for self-control, or exposed to unfortunate combinations of "chance opportunity" do not become seriously and persistently delinquent. Most of those who do engage in serious violative behavior eventually cease doing so—indeed, desistance rather than persistence in delinquency is by far the most common pattern, as can be readily demonstrated empirically (see, for example, Hamparian et al. 1978:72).

The "medical model" so often derided in contemporary discussions of rehabilitation derives from false belief that the necessary task is the identification of some overarching "life problem," its elimination through professional services, and the successful "treatment" of the social pathology termed delinquency. But such direct attack upon basic causes is not invariable in medicine—and is rarely the task of those concerned with the delinquent. It is probably useful to envision the youths of any age group as being composed, at one extreme, of a small proportion who are so subject to a complex of malignant forces as to be almost sure to be delinquent, a small proportion at the other extreme who are almost impervious to opportunity for violative behavior, and a large group in the middle subject to an infinite number of complex personal and situational forces which make it conceivable that they might move toward delinquency under particularly negative conditions.

The reasonable societal task with regard to the delinquent derives from the knowledge that there are within the personalities and within the social situations of most delinquents—or most human beings—healthy margins that can lead to successful social functioning. Emphasizing and drawing these margins into prominence in social functioning and some enlargement of the opportunity structure available to the individual may be expected to tip the scales for considerable numbers of youths engaging in delinquent behavior.

Recent years have seen the emergence of schools of thought—and of practice—defining the task with respect to the offender as stemming from focus upon the immediate problems of social functioning, problems of which the offender is aware and in the solution of which he can be engaged. Thus, those endorsing "behavior modification" tend to be not at all concerned with or even tend to deny the existence of underlying causes, personal or situational. They see behavior only as an ultimately quite rational response to gratifying or aversive stimuli, modifiable by conditioning so that the subject is habituated to positive experience productive of positive behavior. Other schools (such as "task-centered social work," or "reality therapy") take cognizance of personality or situational "life problems" but employ their knowledge as aids in understanding the immediate problems of social functioning confronting the individual, his awareness of the dimensions of his problems, the degree of his motivation to engage in efforts to solve them, his intellectual, emotional, and physical capacities to do so, and the opportunities available or that can be made available to him to do so. The task is seen not as "treating" the individual but as seeking to engage *with* him in the definition of the problem that must be solved if successful social functioning is to be achieved, helping him assess the complexities of the problem and the resources available for its solution, expanding resources when possible, and encouraging effort toward problem solution. From these endeavors we would expect the future's pathways to intervention to emerge.

CHAPTER 4

THE ISSUE OF EFFECTIVENESS

The past two decades have seen much professional literature asserting that empirical tests as well as theoretical speculation have proven the rehabilitative ideal impossible. "Nothing works" has become a byword. Thus, it is asserted, the long quest for means by which the state could intervene positively in the circumstances of hurt and therefore hurtful individuals should be abandoned. The juvenile and criminal justice systems must be oriented to the "more realistic" goals of retribution, incapacitation, and deterrence.

The "Nothing Works" Doctrine

Although outdated, the source still most frequently cited for the "nothing works" doctrine is the review by Lipton et al. (1975) of some 231 reports published before 1967 of correctional program evaluations meeting minimally acceptable standards for research methodology. From this extensive review, Lipton's coauthor Martinson (1974) drew his summary conclusion, which has echoed and reechoed in the professional literature, the journals of opinion, the nation's news and editorial columns, the halls of state legislatures, and the professional conferences and deliberations: "With few and isolated exceptions, the rehabilitative efforts that have been reported so far have had no appreciable effect on recidivism." In clarifying his summary statement, Martinson concluded further that

> these data, involving over two hundred studies and hundreds of thousands of individuals as they do, are the best available and give us very little reason to hope that we have in fact found a sure way

of reducing recidivism through rehabilitation. This is not to say that we found no instances of success or partial success; it is only to say that these instances have been isolated, producing no clear pattern to indicate the efficacy of any particular method of treatment. (Martinson 1974:49)

Martinson's conclusions seemed to find support in the broad overview of results of rehabilitative efforts undertaken by Robison and Smith (1971) as well as the findings of Greenberg's (1977) review of some of the research literature available since the studies drawn upon by Martinson. These and similar reviews contributed to and confirmed the trend of the times. The futility of prevention, treatment, or rehabilitation seemed an almost no longer examined cliché.

However, the very recent era has seen thoughtful questioning of the "nothing works" doctrine. It begins to appear that the doctrine may be an extreme of the typical pattern of pendulum-like swings in the behavioral sciences. Thus Ted Palmer (1975, 1976), one of the researchers most closely involved in the California Department of Youth Authority's I-level programs, reanalyzes the summary report upon which Martinson had based his negative conclusions. Palmer (1976:178) argues that "A careful reading of [Martinson's] article does not warrant this pessimistic forecast. A focus on the actual presence of certain positive findings and relatively optimistic observations and on their significance causes a reassessment of Martinson's sweeping conclusion" (1976:41). Palmer goes on to cite a considerable number of points in the original Lipton et al. survey in which they report projects that appear to have lowered recidivism rates among specified groups of offenders.

In the same more optimistic vein, Ross and Gendreau (1980) report a review of the correctional literature published between 1973 and 1978 and find "a substantial number of correctional treatment programs whose effectiveness has been demonstrated through studies which employed at least quasi-experimental designs and statistical analyses of outcome data" (p. xiii). They note that the available literature "demonstrates that some programs *do* work and have been found to do so in research studies with methodological rigor which matches the best that applied behavioral science has offered in any area" (ibid.). Their book reports upon 23 such studies grouped in five broad modalities: diversion programs, intervention with families of delinquents, community-based programs for juvenile offenders, programs for juveniles in correctional institutions, and programs for adult offenders.

In a further major review, Romig (1978) reports examining 829 evaluation studies and finding 170 meeting the criteria of (1) using either a randomly assigned or a matched control group, and (2) providing measurements of program effectiveness in terms of the subjects' behaviors. Romig finds, as do others, a considerable number of project failures, but also reports a significant proportion of reported successes in achieving altered behaviors. He also provides a summary of the approaches that seem associated with success as well as those apparently associated with failure.

Other scholars cite more isolated but similar findings. Thus, for example, Glaser (1979:210–13) notes a statement by Lipton et al. (1975) that "A clear finding is that intensive probation supervision is associated with reduction in recidivism among males and females under 18 years of age." Glaser also mentions that studies show recidivism reduction through programs enabling prison inmates to maintain family ties through staff-facilitated prison visits, including conjugal visits for married prisoners, as well as through other programs arranging for visits of conventional persons to inmates ordinarily receiving few or no visits (1979:22), and through projects providing "immediate tangible assistance to alleviate released offenders' desperate economic plight" (p. 226).

In sum, the available evidence is confusing—and has, quite naturally, produced bitter disagreement. In response to the widely heralded Lipton et al. survey, Palmer (1975) notes Martinson's emphasis upon negative and underemphasis upon positive reports. Stuart Adams (1976), with his long background of involvement in thoughtful and productive correctional research, concludes that "We have examined the problem of rhetoric in correction and noted that one example—the 'nothing works' doctrine—is a meaningless piece of correctional 'wisdom.' It offers no credible basis for planning, decision making or research in corrections" (p. 90). Martinson (1976) responds that reports of "partly positive results that were reported were akin to a partly pregnant girlfriend—the answers provided by correctional researchers along with 30 cents could buy a cup of coffee in New York." But in a later article, Martinson, after pursuing later reports upon correctional treatment effectiveness, concedes that "On the basis of the evidence in our current study, I withdraw this conclusion [of no effect of correctional treatment programs]. I have often said that treatment added to the network of criminal justice is impotent, and I withdraw this characterization as well. . . . More precisely treatment will be found to be impotent under certain conditions, beneficial under others, and detrimental under still others" (Martinson 1979:254).

It is, perhaps, characteristic of the times that Martinson's earlier allegations of treatment failure still ring through the legislative halls and the professional journals, while his later, much more moderate assessment appeared in a little-remarked law journal article and has inspired little comment. The dispute continues, with more heat than light. As Ross and Gendreau (1980:4) aptly note, "The arguments are persuasive, the rhetoric often brilliant, the metaphors appealing, and the objectivity sadly lacking. The antagonists seem to be more intent on winning arguments than on seeking truth."

It would appear to us that the fact that correctional research should undergo a protracted period of confusion and controversy is not particularly unusual in the long history of the development of ideas. It is not at all uncommon that creative and productive scholars should invest themselves so thoroughly in particular lines of thought as to perceive expressions of disagreement as personal attacks to be responded to with energy and vehemence. Such is the case in most areas of scholarly endeavor. But acknowledgment of confusion is not enough in a field like that of corrections. Offenders will continue to offend, police will continue to arrest, and the justice system will continue to exercise its sway over the lives of thousands of individuals brought within its network. Policies must and will be constantly reshaped. It is vital that generalizations that can be drawn from the present welter of ideas should be made available. And, fortunately, much of what at first seems chaos does make sense when more deliberately considered.

First, let us note that in his earlier central conclusion, narrowly read, Martinson (1974:49) is surely right: "These data . . . are the best available and give us very little reason to hope that we have in fact found a *sure* way of reducing recidivism through rehabilitation" (emphasis added). Could there be—or could there have been even before the survey on which Martinson reports—any other possible conclusion? For most program modalities examined, as many unsuccessful as successful projects can be identified. Even for the apparently most successful programs, the proportion of recidivists remains high. No program can claim that it will succeed with all or almost all subjects, and the proponents of no available methodology can claim that it will, everywhere applied, produce favorable results. Realistically, little else could be expected. The correctional system's task is to cope with problems of little understood origin, with the aid of still primitive theory, employing methodologies still in the process of formulation, in situations in which eventual outcome may be largely determined by variables far beyond the control of the most well-meant endeavor.

Let us further note that most of the rehabilitative projects reported upon have defined their goals in what to today's increasing realism would appear to be hopeless terms. With a limited range of intervention techniques, often employing only one of many available methodologies, they have accepted the responsibility for treating all comers, including undifferentiated groups of offenders of varying personalities, problems, and environmental situations. Subjects often have been drawn into particular programs not because they seem to need specific forms of assistance but because of the methodological bent of a sponsoring agency or program. Some treatment efforts seem to have been skillfully implemented, but others have been so operated as to provoke wonder that any outcome but failure should have been anticipated. Ross and Gendreu (1980:6–7), for example, call our attention to a report of failure on the part of a project heralded as "an exceptionally extensive and experimentally rigorous transformation of the institutional environment." The project was based largely on group counseling. In reality, the counselors implementing the program were lay people with no particular expertise, training meetings for them were poorly attended, training ceased once the program was under way, treatment was not conceptualized or defined in operational terms, the counselors had little faith that their efforts were of any worth, and the counseling group program experienced numerous other problems. But the project is frequently cited as proof that "nothing works."

To further complicate an already wildly complicated task, subjects have quite commonly been drawn into programs attempting to produce change in their attitudes, behaviors, life-styles, and life situations quite without regard to whether they wished to be the targets of intervention. We are only now beginning to realize the frequent futility of such endeavor. We can, perhaps, help some people perceive the probable consequence of failure to change, find hope that change is possible, and become aware of possible sources of help. We may somewhat expand available opportunity. But coerced change in the face of continued lack of desire to achieve it is beyond reasonable expectations.

In spite of the obstacles that must be overcome, an inspiring fact remains: a considerable number of individual projects in the treatment of offenders clearly appear to have produced positive change in the attitudes, ways of life, and proclivities toward violative behavior of many of the human beings who were their subjects. Indeed, how could objective research show otherwise? The social sciences do not yet comprehend how or under what circumstances human growth and behavioral change take place, but that it *does* occur, and that it occurs most often in the presence of human warmth, concern, faith, and dedication to helping surely can not be doubted. We would join with Ross and Gendreau (1980) in asking whether there is any reason to believe that such tendency is common to other human beings but not to delinquents. To us, the most surprising aspect of the reports upon treatment endeavors with delinquents is not that some of them show effectiveness with some subjects, but, rather, that the results should occasion surprise among so many scholars.

It would thus seem to us an enormous loss to the hopes for resocializing badly damaged young people as well as to theory building and knowledge development if we were to cast aside in a tide of "nothing works" philosophy the encouragement readily derived from many recently reported projects. Inspirational examples are available from each major field of practice. The history of the juvenile correctional institution in the United States, for example, has generally been a grim one, too often marked by mindless regimentation punctuated by constant fear of sadistic aggression and sexual attack. But in its Youth Center Project the California Department of the Youth Authority demonstrated that this need not always be so. This project showed that staff can be trained to play meaningful roles in treatment programs. Positive relationships can be developed between staff and youthful inmates. Treatment programs can contribute to more positive inmate views of themselves and their relationships to the world about them. And positive gains can lead to reduced recidivism rates (Jesness 1975).

In juvenile probation, Barkwell (1980) provides a research report demonstrating that assessment of youths' maturity levels on the I-level scale and assignment to officers whose work styles are matched to youths' particular needs can result in improved self-concept, reduced recidivism, and improved school and work attendance. In a small but illuminating voluntary-agency venture, Shore and Massimo (1979) provided vocationally oriented psychological counseling to a group of hard-to-reach delinquent youths with character disorders who had left school. Randomly assigned treatment and control groups were compared at the beginning and the end of the program. The treatment group was shown to have improved to a significantly greater degree than the control group in academic performance, attitudes toward authority, self-image, control of aggression, job performance, and known law-violative behavior. Contrary to usual practice, for this project careful follow-up evaluations were made five, ten, and fifteen years after treatment. It seems quite evident that the project brought lasting change to the lives of its subjects. After fifteen years, the treated group did markedly better than the control group in employment records, stability of family life, utilization of opportunities for continuing education, and freedom from involvement with law enforcement agencies.

Our ability to discern in advance *which* youths will respond positively to what sort of intervention remains at the primitive level, though a few promising efforts have been made. For example, in reports upon the California Community Treatment Projects (Palmer 1974) it appears that the considerable proportion of youngsters referred to the state correctional system who were diagnosed as "neurotics" on the I-level scale tended to make better adjustments if they were referred to community treatment immediately after reception-center diagnosis, while those considered to be at the more immature "power oriented" level on the scale appeared to do better if they first experienced the state's standard, fairly brief correctional institution program. In a sophisticated experiment in the juvenile correctional institution, boys experiencing either carefully developed behavior modification or transactional analysis programs appeared somewhat less likely to recidivate than did those experiencing California's usual, much less systematic institutional programs. However, the two regimes clearly did have differing impacts, with, as would be expected, somewhat greater immediate change being associated with behavior modification and deeper insights and more positive conceptual understanding with transactional analysis (Jesness 1975).

The problem, then, is not a complete absence of rehabilitative models.

Rather, the most difficult problems in implementing the rehabilitative ideal are of a somewhat different order and of three sorts. The first is the relative unpredictability of results even in conscientiously employed programs. The second arises from our dawning realization of the danger of state use of coercive measures designated as rehabilitative but with dreadful frequency proving punitive—often cruelly so. The third derives from limitations in the research methods.

Unpredictability

As we have noted, intervention in the lives of offenders has been shown to be potentially powerful. But it can be destructive if ineptly or inadequately brought to bear. The history of rehabilitative endeavors reveals many projects that have seemed inconsequential, but it also reveals an uncomfortable number that appear to have wrought harm. Experiences such as those of the Cambridge-Somerville Youth Project (Powers and Witmer 1951) are cause for continuing concern. In that oft-cited endeavor, a group of some 500 boys was divided by an unusually impeccable research design into randomly selected experimental and control groups of equal size. Experimental group members were provided with a sort of "Big Brother" relationship by an older, caring person who offered general guidance and counsel, mustered available community services as needed, and was expected to serve as a positive role model. Staff members were from diverse backgrounds, with no particular common professional training. However, they seem to have been sincere and well intentioned and their services were generally positively regarded by their clients.

Thirty years after the conclusion of the Cambridge-Somerville Project, responses to a questionnaire were secured from 113 experimental and 122 control group members, each group having originally numbered 250 (McCord 1978). From their responses, it does not seem that the program was successful in preventing delinquency or crime. Both as juveniles and as adults, equal numbers from both groups had committed crimes. Of those who had committed a first crime, treatment group members were slightly more likely to report having committed a second than were control group members. Perhaps even more disappointingly, in 7 of 57 comparisons related to life adjustment, the control group members surpassed the treated group by slight but statistically significant margins—they were a bit less likely to evidence signs of alcoholism, serious mental illness, or stress-related diseases, and tended to have occupations with higher prestige and to be more satisfied with their work. The treatment group excelled on none of the measures taken.

While better documented than most, the Cambridge-Somerville Project is not unique in appearing to have actually harmed at least some participants. Other instances are available in the literature (see for example Romig 1978). With benefit of hindsight, such phenomena do not seem surprising. Members of a group served by an experimental program may, when questioned at follow-up, show deeper introspection or report more honestly than those participating only in research interviews. Some of the reported "experiments in treatment" clearly provided only the rhetoric of help. Others appear to have operated upon naive assumptions that almost any well-meaning person, even lacking pertinent training or experience, can effectively "counsel" or "treat" or "supervise" delinquent youths. But some more responsibly designed programs may well have encountered more subtle problems. For example, some have been directed at understanding and helping overcome deep-seated feelings that seem to contribute to maladaptive behavior. It would seem possible that such attempts might emphasize and call the feelings into play but be unable to resolve them. Thurber's wry injunction that one is best advised to "Let your mind alone" might have been more apt guidance.

Other dangers would seem apparent. Some programs may succeed in improving self-concept or engendering determination to succeed in positive ways, only to lead to increased frustration and disillusionment when opportunity is lacking. Some youths may deduce from increased attention that they must be "different" from and more problematic than their peers. Some may be labeled by peers and others so that opportunities for positive functioning are foreclosed. In a variety of ways, then, negative "latent functions" of well-intended programs must be guarded against.

Overall program failure is not the only danger confronting the policymaker. In even the most successful programs, in the present state of verified knowledge it is impossible to state *which* youngsters will succeed and which will fail in even the most generally effective intervention program. Experimental tests of program effectiveness have thus far tended to depend upon measurements of success and failure in experimental and control *groups*. One rarely knows what sorts of youths or of problems within such groups yield to interventive efforts and what sorts do not. Only in a few instances—for example, the California Community Treatment Projects (Palmer 1974) or the Youth Center Project (Jesness 1975)—do glimmerings of understanding begin to emerge as to which youths might be more likely than others to respond positively or negatively to a given intervention.

To us, this situation seems likely to continue unchanged in the foreseeable future. Through careful research and experimentation we may be able to improve our ability to calculate rough chances that some as yet only vaguely defined types of youngsters may succeed or fail. We may become able to define more accurately at least the grosser program elements that lead to success or failure. But prediction on an individual basis in all probability will remain a chimera. We work in a field in which it is impossible to measure or to precisely replicate important elements of programs. Examples might be those related to staff members' maturity, sincerity, enthusiasm, interpersonal skills, or similar unmeasurables, each varying in intensity and quality at different times and in differing situations. Further, program impact will vary with an almost infinite variety of subjects' intellectual, volitional, and other subtle personality attributes, as well as with their past, present, and future familial, peer group, and community environments. In the face of such complexities the development of a science of rehabilitation with assured accuracy of prediction would appear remote.

Rehabilitation as Rhetorical Veil

The ambiguities, the uncertainties, the inadequacies of resources that are so evident in efforts to cope with juvenile crime are inevitable sources of insecurity to all who are charged with making the juvenile justice system work. Work with frequently sullen, aggressive, or unresponsive youths can be defeating. Defeat in interpersonal relationships may prove particularly threatening to persons whose self-images are built upon supposed expertise in managing relationships. And correctional employees are charged by the society with somehow managing youths for whose behavior they are expected to be responsible. Anger at

inability to do so may result in punitive controls whose nature is disguised—often almost unconsciously—by rehabilitative rhetoric.

The consequences of such situations are often remote from stated
goals. Thus, youngsters are committed "for their own good" to institutions in which the major life experiences can be sexual and other forms
of aggression, staff indifference, and exposure to powerfully antisocial
values. The cell block structure employed by reform schools to impose
temporary restraint upon recalcitrants is termed the "intensive treatment cottage." Youngsters are incarcerated after having failed in the
community "in spite of all the help given them," when the only actual
service may have been diagnostic study followed by meaningless probation. Cruelty becomes "aversion therapy" and solitary confinement
"meditation."

In sum, then, the present situation is one presenting baffling problems
to the designer of social policy. On the one hand, respectable studies
have demonstrated that it *is* possible to foster growth on the part of
youths functioning in environments seemingly devoid of opportunity.
On the other hand, the outcome of such endeavors is not predictable,
and the possibility of harm is ever present. Most certainly, naive assumptions of former years that rehabilitation could be assured by a
court order and good intentions do not accord with present reality. To
what, then, should we turn? Can we hope that today's naiveté will yield
to firmer understandings enabling surer implementation of proven techniques? The question can be considered only in the light of knowledge
development in the social sciences in general, and in the field of juvenile
and criminal justice in particular.

Methodological Limits Upon Juvenile Justice Research

As we have noted above, flaws in the research upon which much
contemporary rhetoric is based have been a major hindrance in the
pursuit of the rehabilitative ideal. Simply put, researchers have been
necessarily concerned with demonstrating the presence or absence of
causal relationships. Specifically, their interest has been in whether the
introduction of designated treatment approaches can be shown to bring
about measurable changes in behavior. This is a reasonable goal. We

would be irresponsibly shortsighted if we fashioned intrusive interventions into youths' lives without conscientious attempts to monitor the consequences. But decades of experience have demonstrated how difficult it is to test the effectiveness of individual programs.

The design problems that researchers have encountered are not insurmountable in principle. In practice, however, they have proven annoyingly intractable. Random assignment to experimental and control groups—a procedure widely considered necessary in research on causal relationships—ordinarily is not an option, either because local officials cannot be persuaded of its merits, because it seems unfair or morally reprehensible, or because it is simply impractical. As a result, scores of studies have been plagued by methodological liabilities that have limited conclusions about the connection between intervention and outcome. Without a genuine control group and random assignment, it is virtually impossible to rule out the contributions of extraneous factors such as other events in a youth's life or simple maturation. Consequently, our literature is filled with studies that provide considerable information on *correlations* that emerge between interventions and outcome, but that fail to establish the presence of a causal relationship. Though many researchers have resorted to nonexperimental designs, the limitations of these analyses are also acute (Bailey 1982).

As our discussion has indicated, there have been some well-designed studies with adequate controls. But even in these instances—a researcher's nirvana—the results must be taken with a large grain of salt. Many of them conclude, for example, that postintervention comparisons between the performance (however defined) of youths in the experimental and control groups failed to demonstrate statistically significant differences. Such results have understandably led the investigator to conclude that the intervention is not more effective than nonintervention. But this may not be the case. It is reasonable to assume, for example, that many youths assigned to a control group (temporarily or otherwise) are, for one reason or another, being exposed to some form of assistance from a source unrelated to the subject of the program evaluation. Youths who find their way to the program evaluators because they have committed an offense frequently have many needs that are known to other agencies: state departments of social services, clergy, family service agencies, school personnel. Thus, youths in a control group in one study may in fact be under some form of treatment. Consequently, findings of no difference may not mean that nonintervention is as effective as intervention.

Another design issue is related to limits in our ability to generalize the findings of one study to other settings. Only a small proportion of program evaluations have drawn on nationwide samples that are representative of youths in the United States. Because of limitations of funding and the logistical problems associated with designing and managing nationwide studies, most evaluations are restricted to local sites. Every site, of course, has its own idiosyncratic attributes that limit the extent to which researchers and other professionals can generalize results. Thus, the accretion of generalizable knowledge in juvenile justice has been incremental at best, owing to substantial differences in the characteristics of communities, funding arrangements, political climates, treatment approaches, youths, and staff associated with the vast number of programs evaluated. Those who have attempted to tease through the findings on a particular approach have found it difficult to know when a set of results is applicable to their own local circumstances.

A further persistent problem concerns the validity of the variables studied. The intervention frequently lacks precise definition, and it is difficult to know what aspect of a program may have been responsible for observed changes in behavior. For example, a researcher may show that the introduction of a community-based program that includes vocational training, family counseling, and educational upgrading is correlated with lower rearrest rates for participating youths. However, even if we assume that the research design allows the investigator to rule out the influence of extraneous factors (with the use of a control group, random assignment, and so forth), it is ordinarily difficult to know which component of the intervention was responsible for the changes. All three components acting in concert? Two? One? Did the interventions themselves make a difference, or was it merely the personalities of the staff involved that account for the results? Perhaps maturation or simply paying attention to the youths in a sustained and thoughtful fashion was responsible for whatever changes occurred. Thus, the difficulties in measuring or even specifying in precise ways the content of our intervention have severely limited our ability to isolate the specific features of our programs that are responsible for the desirable (or undesirable) changes we document in our various studies.

There is also considerable debate about the adequacy of the outcome measures ordinarily incorporated into program evaluations. It is well known that recidivism rates, based on official police or court records, serve as the most common indicator of outcome in evaluations. By now, however, the use of recidivism rates as the primary measure of effectiveness has a well-documented list of shortcomings. A reduction in recidivism rates is generally considered a very limited indicator of successful outcome following exposure to social services. Changes in youths' attitudes, feelings, aspirations, and relationships may occur as a result of program intervention but may not be reflected in rearrest rates. As any seasoned professional knows, it is not at all unusual for a youth who has made substantial progress following participation in a program to slip up along the way, perhaps to a comparatively minor degree, and be counted as a program failure because of an isolated subsequent arrest. Relatively few juvenile justice professionals who maintain close contact with youths are inclined to automatically consider them failures on the basis of rearrest rates. Conversely, youths who have not been rearrested may have made relatively little progress on whatever problems they are experiencing. Recidivism rates are informative, but they inevitably communicate only a partial story.

Another truism conceded by juvenile justice professionals is that arrest rates—the most common index of recidivism—are poor estimates of the extent of illegal behavior engaged in by juveniles. Arrest rates may tell us more about the professional habits, talents, and biases of police officers than about the incidence of juvenile crime. Though victimization and self-report data also have serious drawbacks, relying on official arrest rates can be particularly misleading.

In addition, available data ordinarily cover only a short period of postprogram time. Owing primarily to the paucity of funds available to support longitudinal research and to the impatience of personnel who are eager to document program outcome, only a small proportion of program evaluations have incorporated follow-up measures beyond one year postintervention. As a result, we have little information about the long-term consequences of our programs. This increases the likelihood that claims about program effectiveness (or failure) reflect false positives (or false negatives). Programs that appear effective in the short run may not have much in the way of lasting consequences (though no doubt many do), and programs that reveal disappointing results in the short run may in fact be responsible for long-term yet undocumented consequences.

These sundry problems all lead up to a variety of difficulties practitioners experience in their efforts to apply research findings to their daily work with juvenile offenders. But a further difficulty stems from the fact that many of the programs that have served as the focus of formal evaluations have lacked clear theoretical formulations to guide them. The vast majority of juvenile justice programs have been based on well-intended efforts to counsel and rehabilitate youths, incorporating a variety of schools of psychotherapy along with the delivery of concrete services. Rarely have programs been designed to test theories of intervention that could be applied across a variety of settings. As Delbert Elliott (1980) has observed,

> Particular program activities and treatment modes have become so institutionalized that they are employed without a clear reference to any particular theoretical paradigm, their own unique theoretical origins having been lost, forgotten, or discredited. They are employed because they have become proper and accepted things to do for youth in trouble, because they are relatively easy to implement, and because people are trained to provide this service or treatment.

As we acknowledged earlier, an additional impediment results from the fact that most program evaluations are based on the analysis of aggregate data collected from groups of youths, while practitioners tend to be interested primarily in the application of results to their work with individual youths. It is simply inappropriate to assume that what holds for the group will hold for each individual within the group (the so-called ecological fallacy). Group or aggregate data are summarized by measures of central tendency (for example, a mean or median) around which there is frequently considerable dispersion. Understandably, then, practitioners as a rule are unable to make direct use of results of program evaluations in their day-to-day activities. Though aggregate data generated by program evaluations have been useful at times for decisions that have needed to be made about policies and strategies for dealing with groups of youths, the difficulty practitioners have had generalizing from these results and extrapolating from them insights relevant to their work with individuals have thus further limited the applicability of research in this area.

But difficulties are also encountered in our efforts to apply research results simply because of genuine disagreements about the meaning of data. It is not at all unusual for two researchers to view identical data and arrive at very different interpretations. Several years ago, for example, the U.S. Office of Juvenile Justice and Delinquency Prevention sponsored a study of alternatives to secure detention for status offenders in Illinois (Spergel et al. 1981). The study included a comparison of recidivism rates for youths who had been provided with noninstitutional alternatives to secure custody (for example, "home detention," temporary foster care, or group home care) and a contrast group of youths placed in secure detention. The findings indicated no statistically significant differences in rearrest rates. Yet professional and lay observers failed to reach consensus about the implications of these data. Do they suggest that secure detention should be preferred over so-called community-based services? "Of course not," according to those who favored the principle of deinstitutionalization. "Of course," asserted those who either believed in the value of incarceration or who were skeptical of noninstitutional programs. The cup was both half full and half empty, one's assessment being dependent upon one's professional vantage point, vested interests, or ideological commitments. The illustration demonstrates the persistence of what the eighteenth-century Scottish philosopher David Hume dubbed the "is-ought" problem (and what G. E. Moore labeled the "naturalistic fallacy"), according to which empirical or descriptive statements of fact cannot be translated directly into normative or evaluative conclusions. As Dwight Ingle (1976:147) noted a number of years ago: "The methods of science are best for determining 'that which is' and 'that which could be,' but they do not suffice for determining 'that which ought to be'."

The State of Our Knowledge

In spite of the wide-ranging problems of design, measurement, and application that have blemished juvenile justice research, we would make an unfortunate error in judgment if we chose to ignore all that we do know from decades of inquiry. Though there are substantial differences of opinion, there is, as we have noted, wide acknowledgment that the results of our efforts to diminish youthful misbehavior have been at best uneven. The combined findings of program evaluations conducted during the past half century reveal a mixed picture: some programs have been shown to be effective with some youths under specified circumstances and with respect to certain measures of outcome. No one intervention or program has been demonstrated effective for all, or almost all, participating youths in all settings and at all times. The success stories have emerged sporadically and for reasons that have frequently eluded discovery. Some programs have been successful, yet our ability to predict for which youths they will be effective, to transfer successful interventions to other youths and settings, and to uncover precise reasons is discouragingly limited. Deep down, we suspect that the outcomes are not random, that both encouraging and discouraging results are a function, at least in part, of our planned and informed program designs. But the actual determinants of outcomes have eluded us.

The results of evaluations of juvenile institutional care have been particularly discouraging. It is well known that institutional life breeds a sustained climate of fear and isolation virtually unmatched in our contemporary world. Tales of predatory acts among inmates abound, in both adult and juvenile facilities, and most are not significantly embellished. They don't need to be. Sexual assault, physical violence, and exploitation thread the lives of many confined in correctional institutions. Though large numbers of inmates are able to skirt institutional violence—because of either their physical stature or their standing in the inmate hierarchy—none are able to escape the omnipotent odor of fear that hangs in the air and is sensed almost immediately by anyone who has walked the corridors and yards of correctional facilities. It is also well known that destructive conflicts regularly and predictably emerge between custodial and treatment staffs, and that youths frequently get caught in the middle. The atmosphere engendered by such conflicts is hardly conducive to genuine treatment.

The results on recidivism are more equivocal. There are claims like Martinson's (1974) that few programs designed for juvenile offenders have demonstrated impressive effects on recidivism. Results of evaluations of institutional and noninstitutional programs are equally debatable (Monahan 1981; Murray and Cox 1979; Coates et al. 1978; Empey 1978; Reamer and Shireman 1981; Empey and Erickson 1972; Empey and Lubeck 1971). Even when positive findings are reported, critical commentary on the study's methodology frequently follows, casting shadows on reports of favorable outcome. The evaluation described earlier of the Community Treatment Project Program of the California Department of the Youth Authority is a paradigmatic example. With unusual methodological sophistication, the evaluators followed randomly selected experimental and control groups to determine the effect of treatment in the open community. A comparison of a control group assigned to one of the CYA institutions with an experimental group whose members were diagnosed and classified by "types" revealed that youths in the community-based program had substantially lower recidivism rates. Following the release of these encouraging results, however, critics argued that the favorable outcome for the experimental group may have been a function of a lower threshold of tolerance for new offenses among regular parole agents (versus the experimental staff). That is, the traditional staff may have been more quick to label as failures youths whose behavior was not significantly different from that of youths in the experimental group (Lerman 1975). However, some doubt is cast upon this conclusion by later data reported by Palmer (1973) and based upon police arrests, rather than parole officer decisions. These data show arrest rates for experimental group boys significantly lower than those for control group boys.

A similar example is provided by the controversial evaluation of the program operated in Cook County (Chicago), Illinois for chronic or serious juvenile offenders—Unified Delinquency Intervention Services (UDIS), a community-based alternative to incarceration. The evaluation entailed a comparison of those in the UDIS program with youths referred to a juvenile institution of the Illinois Department of Corrections, youths on probation, and youths who received court supervision prior to a finding of delinquency. The general finding of this complex study was that large reductions in recorded offenses occurred for youths referred to the correctional institution and those referred to UDIS, though not for youths who received supervision or probation. Further, residential interventions produced significantly larger suppression effects than did nonresidential and court interventions, regardless of a youth's prior offense history. However, these results, which were quickly embraced by those who favored more rather than less intrusive interventions, were almost as quickly assailed by critics who charged that the study suffered from serious methodological flaws. In particular, (1) the apparent suppression effect may have been largely due to the effects of varying rates of attrition among the four groups studied; (2) the observed decline in recidivism may simply reflect maturation of the subjects; and (3) the drop in delinquency rates may have been a function of chance factors, since the youths were selected for treatment as a result of unusually high preintervention rates (what is ordinarily referred to as the problem of statistical regression) (Murray and Cox 1979).

This general climate of controversy has led many practitioners to feel that they have been asked to build a ship in a whirlpool. LaMar Empey (1978:514) has characterized the dilemma well: "From a scientific standpoint, such findings may simply mean that our methods of classifying offenders and of dealing with them are still in a primitive state. We do not know enough about either to make a difference. But, from a practical standpoint, the lack of conclusive findings has simply contributed to the shambles in which the concept of rehabilitation now finds itself."

Given the debatable results that have been produced by the large number of program evaluations conducted to date, what can we hope to gain from the use of scientific tools to assess our efforts to treat juvenile offenders? Is this an ill-fated enterprise representing little more than intellectual gymnastics?

The Pursuit of Knowledge

For decades, social scientists have aspired to the rigor of natural scientists in their efforts to understand human behavior and the effects of interventions designed to alter it. Research methodology has grown more and more sophisticated over the years, moving beyond fascination with experimental and control group design to highly complex mathematical models, multivariate analyses, and the like. We have done our best to construct precise operational indicators of the concepts of interest to us, and we have tenaciously pursued the demonstration of causal relationships among variables. This general trend, of course, has been characteristic of research in criminal justice as well.

The net gain of our enthusiastic brush with empiricism has been disappointing, especially in contrast with the lofty goals we originally set for ourselves. Certainly, the increased sophistication of our research skills and technology has enabled us to gather extensive information about our clients, our agencies, and our payrolls, in less time than has ever before been possible. The range and breadth of data available to researchers almost instantaneously, and the relative speed with which these data can be analyzed with automated equipment, are staggering. Yet for all our sophistication, we know distressingly little about the reasons why juveniles misbehave, ways of changing their behavior, or the effectiveness of various interventions. In part, as we noted earlier, this is due to practical constraints. But our inability to uncover the most basic reasons why people act as they do stems most directly, it now appears, from fundamental limitations in human ability to invent tools to study *themselves* precisely. Our ability to control for hundreds of antecedent and intervening variables when we explore causal relationships; our ability to construct valid and reliable empirical indicators of such concepts as mental health, ego strength, deviance, and self-esteem; our ability to predict future behavior accurately on the basis of retrospective data, all appear severely limited. We have come face to face with what May Brodbeck has referred to as imperfect knowledge:

> Perfect knowledge is the ideal, actualized only in certain branches of physical science. Elsewhere, as in biology, economics, sociology, psychology, and the social sciences generally, knowledge is conspicuously "imperfect." We do not know all the variables that affect, say, a person's resistance to disease, or his behavior under certain circumstances, or the price fluctuations of certain commodities. Our theories in these areas are not complete, nor do we know fully the conditions for closure of such systems. Since we do not know all the factors that make a difference to the variables with which we are concerned, we also have no process laws. From the values of the variables at any *one* time, we cannot predict their value at all other times. (Brodbeck 1968:375).

Our pursuit of perfect knowledge in the social sciences, and in the criminal justice field in particular, has been fueled in a major way by a collective belief that reasons can in fact be found for individuals' behavior and their responses to interventions in their lives: a form of determinism. Yet documentation of determinism in the social sciences has thus far eluded us, leaving us with considerable gaps in our efforts to establish causal chains that lead clearly from antecedent events to outcomes. And this is due partly to a misunderstanding of the nature of determinism in science. Karl Popper observed in his classic essay on indeterminism in quantum and classical physics:

> I suggest that this misinterpretation is due to the tendency of attributing to Science (with a capital S) a kind of omniscience; and that this theological view of science ought to be replaced by a more humanistic view, by the realization that science is the work of ordinary humans, groping their way in the dark. In doing so, we may sometimes find something interesting; we may be astonishingly successful; but we shall never get anything like "the whole truth." Our theories are not descriptions of nature, but only of some little feathers which we plucked out of nature's garb, more or less accidentally. (Popper 1950:193)

If it is indeed the case that our chances of truly uncovering causal explanations of juvenile misbehavior and of producing noncontroversial evaluations of treatment efforts are remote, what functions should we expect research in this field to perform? What knowledge is worth generating?

Research in criminal justice has generally been of three types: explanatory, descriptive, and exploratory. It seems clear by now that we have obtained the least mileage out of explanatory research, that is, research whose goal has been to explain why offenders behave as they do and why our various interventions are or are not effective. This research has produced considerable grist for our intellectual mills, but much of the evidence and the hypotheses derived from it remain conjectural.

In contrast, descriptive and exploratory research has borne considerable fruit. Though the various inquiries have not provided satisfying answers to the most troubling questions in the field (concerning etiology), they have supplied us with valuable information in the "middle range," that is, information that has enhanced the practical design, implementation, and evaluation of treatment programs. Exploratory and descriptive research has expanded considerably what we know about the characteristics of offenders, their offense careers, correlations between offense rates and economic conditions, police practices and behavior, the content and cost of services rendered to clients, the staff who serve them, and, in some instances, program effectiveness. This is undeniably valuable knowledge that ultimately contributes to the effective delivery of services to juvenile offenders, their victims, and the community at large. But we must acknowledge that our most significant gains have been made in this middle range, and that we have fallen far short of our long-standing hope of fully understanding why youths commit offenses and what can be done in response. This is not to degrade the knowledge we have generated after decades of work. It is merely to acknowledge where we have experienced our most substantial gains, and to recognize the apparent limits of our ability to inquire into human behavior and its aberrations.

Does this conclusion imply that we would be wise to abandon the pursuit of a genuine understanding of juvenile misbehavior and ways of treating it? Certainly not. Juvenile crime is a disturbing phenomenon that deeply affects the quality of our lives. What our conclusion of limited success to date does imply is that our goals should be realistic ones. Though it will be important to expend considerable effort toward discovering answers to the most difficult questions associated with juvenile crime—those related to causality—the greatest gains are likely to be found as a result of studies conducted in the middle range. Even here, however, we must be mindful of the limitations imposed by the somewhat primitive nature of our methods of research. Research in the middle range may indeed help us manage the problem; it is not, however, likely to lead to its eradication.

Normal Science and Puzzle-Solving

In his classic dissertation on the nature of scientific revolutions, Thomas Kuhn (1970) observed that a substantial portion of the scientific enterprise is devoted to the pursuit of "normal science" and "puzzle-solving." Normal science, for Kuhn, means "research firmly based upon one or more past scientific achievements, achievements that some particular scientific community acknowledges for a time as supplying the foundation for its further practice" (p. 10). Normal science does not entail ground-breaking research in the sense of fundamental changes in scientists' world view. Rather, it involves refinement of existing research paradigms, much fact-gathering and clarification, but not a scientific revolution. In this sense, much of contemporary science is puzzle-solving; it does not result in major conceptual or theoretical novelties that prove to have great explanatory power. It results, for example, in the further *specification* and *elaboration* of Aristotle's analysis of motion, Ptolemy's computations of planetary position, Lavoisier's application of the balance, or Maxwell's mathematization of the electromagnetic field, rather than the introduction of new theoretical paradigms per se. This work is important, and useful, but it does not result in significant changes in our understanding of our world in the same way that the appearance of the paradigms themselves did.

In these respects, juvenile justice research of the middle range resembles normal science and puzzle-solving. It is important and useful; the knowledge produced by it enhances our efforts at managing our world and its residents. But it does not change drastically our fundamental understanding of our world. As Kuhn noted:

> To scientists, at least, the results gained in normal research are significant because they add to the scope and precision with which the paradigm can be applied. . . . The scientific enterprise as a whole does from time to time prove useful, open up new territory, display order, and test long-accepted belief. Nevertheless, *the individual* engaged on a normal research problem *is almost never doing any one of these things.* Once engaged, his motivation is of a rather different sort. What then challenges him is the conviction that, if only he is skillful enough, he will succeed in solving a puzzle that no one ever before has solved or solved so well. Many of the greatest scientific minds have devoted all of their professional attention to demanding puzzles of this sort. On most occasions any particular field of specialization offers nothing else to do, a fact that makes it no less fascinating to the proper sort of addict. (Kuhn 1970:38)

It is important to acknowledge the potential contributions of research in the middle range in juvenile justice, and it is important not to discourage work that goes beyond normal science and puzzle-solving. But let us also acknowledge what we have thus far learned, that *a genuine scientific revolution, in the Kuhnian sense of that phrase, has not yet appeared on the juvenile justice landscape and is not yet within our range of vision.* In the meantime, much remains to be done with and to be known about youths currently at the court's doorstep. These demands make it incumbent on us to be wise and prudent in the allocation of our research resources and talent, as we strive for that delicate balance between the pursuit of perfect knowledge and inquiry in the middle range. As Aristotle said in his *Nicomachean Ethics:* "It is a mark of an educated man and a proof of his culture that in every subject he looks for only so much precision as its nature permits."

CHAPTER 5
REHABILITATE THE REHABILITATIVE IDEAL?

Earlier, we posed the problem of the development for the juvenile justice system of a vision to work toward. For some several decades, the rehabilitative ideal provided such a vision. But that vision has faded. None of a variety of proposed alternatives wholly satisfies. Procedural justice—"due process"—is a vital but not sufficient means to substantive justice. Retribution plays an inescapable role in defining and supporting societal limits upon behavior, but alone can produce only grim mockery of justice, unappealing to the democratic society hoping to appeal to loftier sentiments. Some necessary degree of societal protection is undoubtedly achieved through deterrence and incapacitation, but the potential for increased protection by manipulation of these is limited at best.

To us, it seems somewhat surprising that the limitations of *any* unitary view of the goals of the juvenile justice system are seldom acknowledged. Scholars and practitioners alike seem to espouse with singular frequency such goals for the rationalization of practice as procedural due process, *or* retribution, *or* incapacitation/deterrence, *or* rehabilitation. True, the temptation to do so is strong. The adoption of a unitary organizing principle for any societal mechanism facilitates mobilization of popular support and orderly, goal-directed administration. But it risks imposing the semblance of order upon a disorderly world. Large social systems are inevitably complex and serve an array of complex goals. So it is with the juvenile justice system. What is needed is thoughtful operationalization of competing values, awareness of the available factual data, and responsible professional judgment to the formidable task of the revision of the juvenile justice concept.

Present discourse regarding substantive rather than procedural issues is sparse. Thus, we begin our efforts to contribute to a conceptual framework for juvenile justice by turning to the thoughtful contributions to adult criminal justice theory and policy made by Norval Morris's (1974) "just deserts" and David Fogel's (1979) "justice" models. These positions rest upon two major principles. The first is a prescriptive principle, which applies the concept of punishment for transgressions. The second is a limiting principle, asserting that coercive intrusion by criminal law should be limited to the situations and degree prescribed by law for the particular offense of which the offender has been found guilty by due process of law. This principle rejects attempts to achieve such social goods as deterrence, incapacitation, rehabilitation by applying sanctions more rigorous than those statutorily provided for the offense leading to conviction.

We accept these two principles as partial—but only partial—guides to juvenile justice policy.

The prescriptive principle expresses the assumption necessary to the preservation of the social fabric: that behavior is generally in large part volitional. The connection between behavior and its consequences must be maintained. Thus will law-conforming behavior be encouraged and law-violative behavior discouraged. The law will exercise its teaching, moralizing function; and thus also will be assured the retention of the justice system as the instrumentality through which society expresses the retributive thrust arising from resentment and fear of the offender and rejection of behavior defined as crimes.

Complementing the prescription of punishment is the limiting principle. This principle would rule out attempts to use state authority to curb the offenders's freedom beyond those arising incidental to the administration of the degree (and only the degree) of punishment prescribed by law for the specific offense. Such provision is of particular importance in a time when what Francis Allen (1981) and others have termed the "war theory" of justice is prevalent in the land. Calls for "war on crime" are common. Offenders are defined as the enemy, a different order of human being, "scum," to be removed from society at all costs. The call is to make an example, to "get him off the streets." The impossibility of distinguishing between those who will and will not continue to offend is not recognized, nor is the enormous social cost of institutionalizing the considerable proportion of our juvenile population that one would have to deal with in order to achieve any significant degree of added societal protection.

The limiting principle would protect against the abuses that have too often resulted from the presence of the rhetoric of rehabilitation without its substance. Youngsters could no longer be subjected to the coercive power of the state for longer periods than those prescribed by law for their offense records. The Gerald Gaults of America could no longer be made subject to state control for seven years for making an indecent phone call.

Our quarrel, then, is not with the contribution that the "just deserts" or "justice" models can make to the quest for justice for the child. But we live in an era characterized by calls for "grown-up penalty for grown up crime." Such is the philosophical basis undergirding moves toward habitual offender laws, automatic transfer to criminal court for increased ranges of offenses, presumptive sentences and "sentencing grids" for juveniles, and demands that the juvenile court process be rigidly defined as adversarial in nature or that the juvenile court simply be eliminated. In this climate, it may not be realized that retributive models can carry us only part of the way toward substantive juvenile justice. Thus, we next address ourselves to the task of defining what more must be added to retributive theory if substantive justice is to be achieved. Unless this is done, the comforting assumption that justice resides in fair determination of guilt or innocence and the passionless attachment of a penalty to guilt is too readily available. We fear the danger of erring in a manner quite like that of which the rehabilitationist is so frequently accused: the use of rhetoric to obscure practices with latent functions defeating intended consequences.

Underlying narrow interpretations of retributive models—interpretations not included in the writings of the models' progenitors but nonetheless common—is the assumption that the justice system must act as if its functionaries believed that everyone is relatively equally capable of free choice among a range of conforming or nonconforming behaviors. But that is not the case in the real world. Gross disparities exist in available social, economic, and other opportunities to select conventional behaviors. Because of their immaturity or of the circumstances of their rearing, juveniles in particular may not have wholly developed capacities to perceive the full array of choices or the consequences of each. The choices they do make may be the result of long histories of injustice against them. Their behavior may be a blind lashing-out against a rejecting world or a cry for help born of desperation.

For these reasons, we note with satisfaction the recent appearance in criminological literature of indications that the pendulum is swinging back to a more central position, on both sides of the Atlantic. A rising British philosopher-scholar of the criminal justice scene summarizes his position in a way expressive of major aspects of our own:

> Policies which ignore the social and economic realities in which children find themselves, while promoting greater equality and justice within formal systems of control, may not only ignore but may compound the structural and material inequalities which have historically been associated with criminal behavior. The provision of justice for children will require a fundamental reappraisal of the life opportunities offered to children. Increased protection within systems of control may promote children's rights procedurally but may fail to recognize them substantively. It may also abrogate our responsibility to meet those rights. To do so would be unjust. (Asquith 1983b:17).

The Role of Rehabilitation

From the above paragraphs, the prescriptive aspects of the "just deserts" and the "justice" models, with their emphasis upon punishment related to severity of offense, are, as would be granted by their framers, important but not adequate guides for policymakers or practitioners. The hope for a single lodestar vanishes. We are left with a neverending series of demanding judgments calculated to harmonize differing values. Retribution remains a valid purpose, but so do both general deterrence and incapacitation. And even these are not enough. Our concern for substantive justice leads us to include among essential functions the provision to youths of help toward "rehabilitation," "reintegration," "solution of problems of social functioning," or whatever euphonious term may be desired. Thus we would continue to impose upon the juvenile court the responsibility for inquiry into the antecedents of delinquent behavior and the provision of, or the enabling of provision through other resources of feasible help in growing toward positive social functioning.

As we have noted throughout, we are quite aware of the manner in which the rhetoric of rehabilitation has in the past disguised endeavors that have been grossly unrealistic or actually harmful. We are aware of the risk of corruption of the treatment process. We do not believe that the democratic society in good conscience can deprive the child and/or his family of the right to determine their own lives for the purpose of imposing rehabilitative treatment, in the face of our dubious ability to predict results. This conviction leads us to a purpose a major element of which is well encapsulated by one of Norval Morris's many felicitous phrases, "facilitated, rather than coerced change." But we would further strengthen the concept by adding to our vocabulary a term paraphrased from Cullen and Gilbert (1982:266): "obligatory opportunity." We refer, of course, to the obligation on the part of the state to seek substantive justice for the young person by offering the opportunity to grow toward responsible citizenship. We consider the pathway toward the rehabilitative ideal to run through the use of the finest of professional skill and dedication in providing the *offer* of help. Such offer would extend to "reaching out" to the child and family so as to demonstrate depth of concern and to help them perceive and move toward use of alternatives available to them, in the light of knowledge of the probable consequences of each. We would continue to require of the child the normal performance obligations and behavioral restrictions imposed by the society on all children. But acceptance or rejection of help would remain with the child and family—not the court or the other elements of the justice system. This perspective would, we believe, do much to avoid abuses of authority. And, far from incidentally, our proposal would do much to create a sort of "buyer's market" in personal services. Providers of services would have to orient themselves to their prospective clients' perceptions of problems, offer help perceptible to potential recipients as meaningful, and elicit clients' own investment in the problem-solving process. Current understanding of the nature of the helping process suggests that such is the only generally feasible pathway to the promotion of change.

Present understandings also suggest that the offer of noncoercive help need not be an exercise in futility. Within the personalities of most of us—including most offenders—there do reside healthy thrusts toward personal growth, toward achievement of the potentials of the self, toward contributions to others, and toward striving for positive recognition from others. It is the identification of these and the enhancement of opportunity for operationalizing them with which we are here concerned.

In sum, then, we would maintain the goal of rehabilitative opportunity as essential to the operation of a juvenile justice system. But we do not believe that rehabilitation will ever regain the central theoretical role that it once held. Rehabilitation should and will remain an important goal of juvenile justice—but only one of several competing goals, no one of which is sufficient to determine the state's orientation to the juvenile offender. The justice system must energetically assert society's rejection of offense behavior and the possibility of a punishment for such behavior. To the extent possible, it must do so in a manner that deters others from offending. It must incapacitate those who have offended most heinously, thus, perhaps, averting at least some repetitions—*and* it must provide opportunity for growth toward eventual full membership in the law-abiding community.

Rehabilitation as here defined cannot supplant other justice system responsibilities; it can only supplement them. In a sense, it will be incidental to them. The youngster may, for example, be committed to the juvenile correctional institution as a means of upholding the power of the law. A degree of general deterrence and of incapacitation will result. The institution will have the responsibility of holding him securely in decent custody for the interval prescribed by law and by order of the court. But as a central aspect of performing that function, the institution will also bear the responsibility of providing the youngster with opportunity for learning and for growth toward reentry into the free community. The provision of opportunity will not be the reason for the existence of the institution. However, in very real part, it will dictate the manner in which the institution discharges its function of holding in secure custody. And in its discharge of its rehabilitative endeavors the juvenile justice system will most directly express the democratic society's essential commitment to the concept of the worth of the future citizen.

We close our argument on this point with a quotation from, of all persons, Willard Gaylin and David Rothman, two of today's most vocal proponents of the retributive rather than the rehabilitative model. We find their sense of loss deeply moving: "in giving up the rehabilitative model, we abandon not just our innocence but perhaps more. The concept of desert is intellectual and moralistic; in its devotion to principle it turns back on such compromising considerations as generosity and charity, compassion and love" (Gaylin and Rothman 1976, quoted in Cullen and Gilbert 1982:249). We fear that many sincere proponents of the retributive model remain innocents in their grasping for a single, easy solution to the disturbing problems of today's criminal justice system. In their innocence they tread a path very probably leading to more, not less, injustice and to more, not less, repression. And we would fear even more the borrowing of this philosophy to apply to the juvenile justice system.

The Dispositional Process

The possible operationalization of the broad principles enunciated above can best be illustrated by examining case disposition in the juvenile justice system, for it is about the dispositional process that the system's functions revolve. Our vision of the manner in which the process might operate owes much to the work of two distinguished work groups, each having given months of study to the issues involved: the Juvenile Justice Standards Project of the American Bar Association's Institute of Judicial Administration (IJA-ABA 1977), and the Twentieth Century Fund's Task Force on Sentencing Policy Toward Young Offenders (1978).

Our recommendations also rest heavily upon two assumptions. First, as we have previously noted, we assume that the juvenile court will have original jurisdiction over all felony-type offenses on the part of juveniles but will waive to the criminal court jurisdiction over *a very few* offenders either (1) accused of a crime or series of crimes so violent and so outrageous as to demand unusually protracted and secure incarceration, or (2) accused of very serious crimes and having previously experienced the total range of sanctions available to the juvenile justice system.

The second assumption upon which our sentencing framework rests is that the time span of youth is much shorter than that of an adult. A total developmental stage may run no more than three or four years and if not then successfully negotiated may never be wholly achieved. To the adult, years pass with rapidly accelerating tempo; to the youth, a year may seem to stretch into infinity. The achievement of suitable punishment and of general deterrence among the juvenile population will call for plans involving shorter time spans than is the case when dealing with adults.

It will also be noted that we do not here discuss issues concerning the application in juvenile court of the due process protections supposedly provided in the criminal court. We have earlier expressed our belief that such protections are a precious part of our heritage and that there is no fundamental reason for not making them available in the juvenile court. Recent years have seen remarkable progress toward this end. The remaining task regarding them is largely one of implementation.

The problem looming on today's social policy horizon is the disposition by the juvenile court of delinquency cases. We suggest that it necessitates a twofold decision-making process: first, to what extent, if any, does the committing offense, considered in connection with any prior offense record, so arouse societal condemnation as to demand the imposition of a coercive sanction; and, second, to what extent is it necessary and feasible for the state to mobilize any available resources enhancing the youth's opportunity to grow toward citizenship?

The Least Restrictive Alternative

In keeping with our earlier comments concerning the unpredictability of results of and the dangers associated with coercive intervention, the above decisions should be governed by the requirement urged by the American Bar Association Institute of Judicial Administration (IJA-ABA 1977:34): "In choosing among statutorily permissible dispositions, the court should employ the least restrictive category and duration of disposition that is appropriate to the seriousness of the offense, as modified by the circumstances of the particular case, and by the age and prior record of the juvenile. The imposition of a disposition should be accompanied by a statement of the facts relied on in support of the disposition and the reasons for selecting the disposition and rejecting less restrictive alternatives."

Fixed Maxima

As a further principle governing the dispositional process, we would suggest abandoning the long-established juvenile court reliance upon almost completely indeterminate sentencing to a dispositional category arrived at by equally complete judicial discretion. Juvenile courts have traditionally exercised enormous dispositional authority. Even a minor offense can result in commitment to the state correctional system. In most states, the duration of such commitment is limited only by the provision that youths pass from the jurisdiction of the juvenile court upon attaining their majority: commonly age 21. True, youngsters are usually retained in institutions for periods much shorter than those possible. But the length of retention is at the discretion of the state, and even after release, state supervision may continue for years.

Wholly satisfactory resolution of this problem is difficult. However, it is becoming increasingly widely agreed that *the maximum duration of all coercive dispositions should be determined at the time of sentence.* We would envision such a purpose as being implemented by a system in which:

1. Maximum sentences for broadly defined classes of offenses would be established by statute;

2. The court would fix maximum sentences within the statutorily established maxima;

3. Commitment to nonsecure residential care or other nonsecure sanctions would be reviewable at any point, either upon the petition of any receiving facility or agency or upon the motion of the court; and

4. Commitment to secure correctional facilities would be through a central state authority—typically the department responsible for juvenile corrections—which would be empowered to release to supervision within the community for the remaining duration of sentence at a date short of the maximum.

The system proposed here is essentially that proposed by the Twentieth Century Fund study group (1978:12). It resembles present practice in many states, with one major exception: the fixing of maxima.

Classification and Duration of Disposition

The "least restrictive alternative" philosophy achieves substance only when coupled with suggested definitions of alternatives. In the present state of social policy regarding the delinquent, definitions are in the process of development. Different states will experiment with differing formulations. Eventually, degree of consensus greater than presently available should emerge. We would recommend that it be along lines resembling those suggested by the IJA-ABA (1977:40–47). Their recommended standard envisions three classes of disposition:

1. *Custodial,* by which the juvenile is either ordered confined in a secure facility or placed in a nonsecure residential facility or foster home;

2. *Conditional,* by which the juvenile is released, but upon condition that he remain under probation supervision, or make restitution, or undergo a similar sanction short of a change of residence; or

3. *Nominal,* by which the juvenile may be reprimanded, warned, or referred to other voluntary services, but is unconditionally released.

The same standards propose that offenses be graded by utilizing classifications established by criminal statutes but attaching to them less severe—or at least less protracted—penalties than those provided in criminal law. Thus they envision a scale of offenses and maximum penalties that may be summarized as follows (recalling that a juvenile court finding of an exceptionally heinous offense or of a hardened juvenile offender over the age of 15 may result in waiver to criminal court):

Class One Offenses (those for which at criminal law, maximum sentences include death or imprisonment for 20 years or more): custodial sanction up to 24 months or conditional freedom for 36 months;

Class Two Offenses (at criminal law permitting imprisonment for from 5 to 20 years): custodial sanction up to 12 months or conditional freedom for up to 18 months;

Class Three Offenses (at criminal law permitting imprisonment for from 1 to 5 years): custodial sanction for up to 6 months or conditional freedom for up to 18 months;

Class Four Offenses (at criminal law permitting imprisonment of from 6 months to 1 year): secure custody for up to 3 months *if the juvenile has a severe prior record,* nonsecure custody for up to 3 months, or conditional freedom for up to 12 months;

Class Five Offenses (at criminal law permitting imprisonment for 6 months or less): nonsecure custodial care for up to 2 months or conditional freedom for 6 months.

The above scale is one with which one might differ in detail but that establishes the sort of "ball park" we have in mind. However, it deals with maxima. In doing so, it does not emphasize an aspect of reality that we consider essential: *a considerable proportion, probably more than half of all juvenile offenses, can be dealt with informally (without the filing of a formal petition with the court, or with dismissal of such petition by informal action at a preliminary screening stage), or should result in dismissal by the court after reprimand and warning.* For many juveniles, reliance can best be placed upon the shock of arrest, warning, very temporary prehearing detention if this has been found necessary, and/or referral to other community services that seem indicated. An enormous proportion of juvenile offenses do not necessarily predict further delinquency and do not constitute serious threats to public safety. For such cases, refraining from stigmatization and, incidentally, avoiding flooding the court with a sea of unnecessary cases become desirable goals.

Proportionality

Admittedly, a sanctioning scheme limiting discretion only by setting maxima does not ensure "proportionality." Proportionality is a term seldom precisely defined (and, in criminal justice, perhaps undefinable) which as it is most frequently used appears to include two concepts. The first envisions sanctions somehow commensurate with the gravity of the offense involved. This is a concept almost impossible to operationalize, as gravity of offense and severity of sanction must necessarily be measured, to the extent that they are measurable, on two different scales, whose relationship cannot readily be established. The second concept is that of sanctions proportionate in severity to each other— "like sanctions for like offenses." But the difficulties involved in determining when two offenses are alike are not solved by grouping them together under some statutory nomenclature. "Aggravated assault" charges resulting from a schoolyard fight refer to a quite different reality than does a similar charge involving a mugging. There are an undefinable number of kinds of aggravated assault. Further, each kind takes on meaning only within its context. Thus, the true "seriousness" of the offense must be assessed in terms of such variables as the injury done the victim, the degree of intent involved, the degree of any provocation, the age and maturity of the offenders and their emotional states. No penal code can encompass all the factors necessary to meaningful measurement of severity. And even if it could, account would still have to be taken of the fact that different punishments will have differing weights for different offenders. Some youngsters will be painfully punished by mere arrest and identification as offenders. Others will not. To some, six months in a juvenile correctional institution is an indescribable horror; others "can do six months in a breeze."

Still another confounding factor is that the elimination of discretion at one point in a long and involved process may merely shift it to another point. Police and state's attorneys know very well the probable results of various charges—and they do not hesitate to use discretion in charging when confronted by a legal code so rigid as to make it difficult for the court to consider important variables. They are free to exercise their prerogative on the basis of personal predilection, ambition to achieve an impressive conviction record, or other purpose unanticipated by statute. Their actions may result from relatively private decisions quite free of public due process.

In sum, we are aware of the horrendous stories to be told of the results of unbridled judicial discretion. We agree with the abstract goal of government by law, not by the varying whims of fallible people. But we believe that the greatest societal advantage is achieved by statutory definition citing (1) the justification of sanctions as being the preservation of the power of the law to maintain the consequences of behavior, (2) the principle of adoption of the least restrictive alternative, (3) the curbing of discretion by the establishment of maxima, (4) the requirement that the dispositional order cite the ground and the reasons why a specific sanction rather than one less restrictive was adopted, and (5) the establishment of responsibility on the part of the court to inquire into the nature of any rehabilitative service indicated and, when possible, to assure the offender of such service.

We fear that the more rigid sentencing schemes, enacted in the hope of achieving justice, may breed greater injustices of their own. Under them, commensurability and proportionality are too often legal rationalizations making it possible to avoid the troubling task of grappling with the problem of the relationship between offense and sanction. We are aware that no wholly satisfactory solution exists to the problem of reconciling the thrust toward justice as represented by visible and evident proportionality, on the one hand, and justice as shaped by the infinite variability of the human condition, on the other. We strive, then, for the least unsatisfactory solution. We hope that the future may reveal less tortuous paths to justice than those now evident.

Expanded Dispositional Alternatives

Any model such as that we suggest will make necessary a wider range of dispositional alternatives than that available to most juvenile courts. Very generally, courts have three broad alternatives. They may dismiss charges. They may return the offender to the community under probation supervision. Or, they may employ a custodial disposition: usually, commitment to a state juvenile correctional institution. Dismissal or probation may be accompanied by referral to other services, which will be meaningful to many youths. But to many, return to the community will seem a "pass": the equivalent of no action. As we noted earlier, to such youths the experience will suggest little more than that society and its agents are either impotent or easily hoodwinked. But the other choice, institutional commitment, is a long step along the restrictive continuum, may be harsher than desired, and presents real dangers of criminalization. The need is for an expanded range of "in-between" dispositions enabling firm state action short of incarceration in a correctional institution. The need is considerably heightened by the responsibility of the court to seek ways of expanding youths' opportunities to grow toward citizenship.

Recent years have seen at least a beginning basis of a considerable range of dispositional alternatives. Most have been demonstrational or experimental; many have been funded as such by the U.S. Office of Juvenile Justice and Delinquency Prevention. Many have been short lived. A fairly adequate literature is available on them, and we summarize the current state of the art in this area in chapter 6. Most are best employed in conjunction with release from court supervision. However, one group of programs requires particular mention here as it usually involves continued court supervision and is often employed as an official disposition. We refer to the many recent projects calling for various forms of restitution. Of all the range of current programs, those involving restitution, either in the form of direct payment or service to victims or in the symbolic form of community service, appear to us to be most capable of capturing the imagination of policy planners and to offer the most hope for development.

Of course, restitution has long been employed at least occasionally in U.S. juvenile courts. But an occasional restitution order, unstudied, unevaluated, and with little support to make it effective does not constitute a meaningful exploration of the option. More systematic exploration has been inaugurated in the United States only in the very recent years and is still under way (see, for example, Schneider et al. 1982). Thus far, it appears that restitution programs have the potential for attaching a realistic consequence to offense behavior while reducing the occasions for incarceration. Restitution orders may also foster a sense of responsibility in juveniles, provide opportunity for expiation and relief of guilt, and promote community confidence in the juvenile justice process. And in at least some of its applications, restitution may provide a gesture toward justice for that most ignored participant in the crime scenario: the victim.

Restitution may take a variety of forms: monetary, direct service to victims, unpaid community service, paid employment enabling monetary restitution, or a combination of these alternatives. Of these, the form that appears to us to be most promising for wide-scale development is unpaid community service. Direct monetary restitution to victims is sometimes a desirable goal, but one applicable to only a small proportion of cases. Few juveniles involved in crime and delinquency have significant monetary resources. Paid employment for them is usually difficult to arrange. And very often the last thing the victim desires is any further contact with offenders. "Symbolic restitution" in the form of community service may afford most of the advantages of other restitution programs and may be implemented on quite large scale.

In Great Britain and Germany, community service has long been a major dispositional alternative, and the programs are generally more sophisticated than in the United States. In those countries it is common for regularly assigned staff units from local child welfare or social welfare departments to bear the responsibility for developing and supervising work placement resources. Youths ordered by the courts to perform community service are referred to these units, where careful assignment is made, youths' discharge of their responsibilities is checked, and reports back to courts are made.

We are concerned lest community service become a fad, with poorly planned and poorly supervised projects springing up haphazardly, inevitably failing, and resulting in disillusionment. We are also concerned lest they become employed in a manner so as to retain under state control new groups of minors not previously subject to continuing authoritative intervention in their lives. We do not think community service projects should be justified on the basis of their teaching work habits, or providing prevocational training, or in other ways being rehabilitative. We believe their primary function to be that of maintaining the law's emphasis on the relationship between behavior and its consequences and the law's assurance to the community that something is being done about behavior defined as threatening the property and person of the citizen. When community service has been ordered for such purpose, its ancillary, possibly rehabilitative functions may productively be explored.

The Confusing Status of the "Status Offender"

Our focal concern thus far has been the "heavy" delinquent: the youngster whose offense constitutes a danger to the person and/or property of his fellow citizens. But much of the energy of the juvenile justice system—and much of the controversy surrounding it—involves concerns arising from the court's jurisdiction over quite a different complex of behaviors: those illegal on the part of children but not constituting crimes when performed by adults. No commentary upon the contemporary juvenile justice scene can avoid at least passing reference to the current, often impassioned debate concerning suitable social policy regarding that conglomerate of truants, runaways, children failing to respond to parental supervision, or otherwise at war with their families or within themselves whom we term "status offenders."

The debate is of relatively recent origin. For several decades after the founding of the juvenile court, all juvenile law offenders were simply "delinquents." Illustrative of the wide sweep of the omnibus definitions of delinquency in most states was the South Dakota Juvenile Court Act, current for half a century and not repealed until 1968. It brought under the jurisdiction of the court, to cite only a few of its provisions,

> Any child who, while under the age of 18 years, violates any law of this state or any ordinance of any city or town of this state; who is considered incorrigible, or intractable by parents, guardian, or custodian; . . . who, without cause and without the consent of its parents, guardian, or custodian absents itself from its home or place of abode; who is growing up in idleness or crime; who fails to attend school regularly without proper reason therefore . . . but loiters and idles away its time; who knowingly frequents or visits a house of ill repute . . . or any saloon or dram shop where intoxicating liquors are sold; . . . or who wanders about the streets in the nightime without being on any lawful business or lawful occupation; . . . or jumps or attempts to jump into any moving train; . . . or writes or uses vile, obscene, vulgar, or profane, or indecent language or smokes cigarettes or uses tobacco in any form; . . . or who is guilty of indecent, immoral, or lascivious conduct. . . . (Quoted by Rubin 1979:37–38)

While the above prescription may be more detailed than most (though not extremely so), its spirit duplicates that of the laws of most states. The juvenile court's concern is not only with the youngster who is in some way at war with society; it is also with the youngster who offends against prevailing standards of propriety. And in order to be sure that any such child might be brought into the court's hopefully benevolent network, jurisdictional bounds are usually writ so large as to include behaviors at some time or another indulged in by almost all youths.

The juvenile court's jurisdiction over status offenses is so widely invoked as to constitute a major proportion of the court's workload. That proportion probably peaked in the mid-1970s. Thus, Krisberg and Schwartz (1983:341) note that in 1975 the nation's juvenile courts disposed of 1,406,100 cases. Of these, 335,600, or slightly less than one-fourth, involved status offenses. No detailed analysis is avilable on the impact of the court experience upon the youngsters involved in these cases. However, it can hardly have been trivial. Surprisingly, the youngster referred to the court on the basis of a status offense was considerably more likely to be placed in detention than were those involved in behaviors generally considered more truly delinquent. Thus 43 percent of the status offense cases for that year but only 18 percent of the property offense and 26 percent of the person offense cases involved detention.

By the mid-1970s, however, heated debate had arisen as to whether such widespread exercise of the "parens patriae" function of the state by an agency at least closely related with the criminal justice system should be considered, on balance, to provide to its subjects a benign or a criminalizing experience. The data necessary to answer the question did not exist then and do not exist now. More precisely, we do not know which status offenders may be expected to respond how, to what sort of authoritarian intervention by the state into their lives and the lives of their families. The absence of such knowledge, combined with extremely dim prospects that it will be generated in the foreseeable future, suggests to many the need to limit to an absolute minimum the situations in which the state is empowered to intervene coercively in status offender cases.

The last assumption is strengthened by the Anglo-American tradition that the primary responsibility for inculcating societally approved standards of behavior is that of the family. Thus, obedience at home, attendance at school, avoidance of possible corrupting influences, and the like, are essentially family responsibilities. But recognition of this generally held value does not necessarily lead to the assumption that the juvenile court's jurisdiction over status offenses is either intrinsically evil or misguided. It does not establish that the use of the power of the state to reinforce family authority is *always* inherently wrong. Parents' attempts to exercise their training, guiding, protecting role are frequently obstructed by powerful peer group, sociocultural, economic, or other forces beyond the control of the family. Some youths are so obdurately rebellious as to demand some form of "rescue" attempt simply out of humane concern for their eventual welfare. The negative behavior of some is clearly the result of parenting practices so lax or so wrong as to necessitate some form of external intervention.

The issue currently widely agitated is not so much whether the state should be prepared to extend support to the troubled child from a troubled family; rather, the question is whether this can effectively be done by so formal an apparatus as the juvenile court and justice system.

The emerging preponderance of opinion among legal scholars seems to be that it cannot. Thus, the IJA-ABA Juvenile Justice Standards project group says (1977:4, 11): "It is widely conceded that unruly child cases are usually the most intractable and difficult matters with which the juvenile court has to deal," and goes on to remark that "Using legal compulsion to restore (or provide) parent-child understanding and tolerance and to build up mechanisms for conflict resolution within the family unit is akin to doing surgery with a spade."

We are not so sure that the problem is so impossible as it is painted. We suspect that the average delinquency case, from which the court does not shrink, poses intrapsychic, intrafamilial, and social adjustment problems quite as complex and confusing as those of the status offender. In fact, we are impressed by the findings of a fair number of careful studies the evidence from which is to the effect that it is difficult to determine whether status offenders are inherently different from delinquents (these studies are well summarized by Hellum and Peterson 1983:84–92). And we have consistently argued that most helping endeavors, with whomever they are undertaken, must be undertaken by the skilled opening of the door to voluntary participation in problem resolution. Many endeavors of this kind are carried out by agents of the court and justice system. And, as we have noted above, the familial and societal problems associated with status offense cases do not infrequently necessitate the availability of some form of state intervention to protect the rights of the child or the parent or both.

To us, therefore, the task of building social policy does not seem to be simply that of terminating the status offense jurisdiction of the juvenile court. Rather it is one of retaining the potential for intervention when necessary, *while curbing the possibility of abuse of authority.* That such abuses are common, we are keenly aware. The literature and our own observations reveal clearly the frequency with which hurt, angry, frightened families encounter, in the commonly overloaded bureaucracy of the big-city juvenile court, a harassed judge who in a brief hearing precipitously and too often arrogantly orders the life situation of uncomprehending family members. (See, for example, the study by Linn et al. 1979 on the treatment of status offenders in one major metropolitan juvenile court.) We are offended, but not surprised, by the fact that two national studies have shown, respectively, that in the mid-1970s 33 and

35 percent of all inmates of juvenile correctional institutions were status offenders (Hasenfeld 1976:67). Apparently, if left to exercise their powers unchecked, many juvenile court judges are quite as likely to send young truants or runaways to institutions as they are to send recidivist robbers. True, the truant or runaway may be just as "disturbed," just as aggravating, and just as much a possible threat to society or to himself as is the robber. *If* one were to accept a premise that the correctional institution functions as a therapeutic agent—a sort of "hospital" for those experiencing problems in adjustment to society—one could accept its general use as means of treating status offenders. But we do not accept that premise. Earlier we made clear that we believe the only justification for commitment to the correctional institution is the upholding of the law's capacity to protect society from the offender whose behavior has injured the citizen or usurped property. The correctional institution is not a hospital.

As further grounds for seeking policy limiting (though not abrogating) the juvenile court's jurisdiction over status offenders, we believe that the major thrust of all endeavors on behalf of this group should come from the institutions in which the youngsters' problems originate and in which they are manifested: the family, the school, and other community forces. By keeping an open door for status offense cases, the court permits itself to be used as an easy "solution," thus weakening the drive on the part of families, schools, and social agencies to solve problems that only they can ultimately solve. Thus Rubin (1979:51–52) aptly quotes David Bazelon, a distinguished federal judge, addressing the 1970 Convention of the National Association of Juvenile Court Judges to the effect that "The situation is truly ironic. The argument for retaining beyond control and truancy jurisdiction is that juvenile courts have to act in such cases because 'if we don't act, no one else will.' I submit that precisely the opposite is the case: because you act, no one else does. Schools and public agencies refer their cases to you because you have jurisdiction, because you exercise it, and because you hold out promise that you can provide solutions."

We need to consider strategies other than unabridged authority by the juvenile court to intercede in the life and family situation of the status offender. The most commonly cited proposals call for *deinstitutionalization, diversion,* and *divestment.*

Deinstitutionalization and Diversion

As doubts about the conception of the correctional institution as a helping, healing institution became more insistent in the 1960s, the frequently punitive, too often brutalizing nature of such institutions became more widely recognized. Consequently, doubts arose about the propriety of committing to them youngsters whose "offenses" had been an inability to respond to the supervision of the family and the school—supervision which often seemed grossly inadequate or misdirected. The fault is not *always* the child's. The first step taken by several states to respond to this growing awareness was to modify the omnibus definition of delinquency. Delinquents were defined by statute as only those youths who had committed offenses that constituted crimes if committed by adults. New terms were devised to define status offenders statutorily: "minors," "persons," or "children" "in need of supervision" (thus "Mins," "Pins," or "Chins"), for example. In most states in which these new definitions were created, the youngsters involved remained under the jurisdiction of the juvenile court, as before, and might be treated much the same as before, with one important exception: they could no longer be committed to institutions for delinquent youths, or commitment could take place only under defined exceptional circumstances. Some states forbade the use for such youngsters of preadjudication detention. Thus, according to Kobrin and Klein (1983:35) by 1975 some 14 states had in various ways and to various degrees prohibited commitment to correctional institutions and 5 had forbidden preadjudication detention. This movement was powerfully accelerated by 1974 legislation (amended and somewhat clarified in 1977) making states not having forbidden placement of status offenders in institutions for delinquents ineligible for federal funds under the large-scale grant-in-aid programs administered by the U.S. Law Enforcement Assistance Administration.

The full effect of these endeavors is difficult to measure. Apparently, their greatest impact was upon policies governing the admission to institutions of female status offenders. Thus, between 1974 and 1979 admissions to detention in the United States declined by 12.3 percent, or 77,265 fewer admissions. Eighty percent of this decline resulted from reductions in admissions of females, who are most commonly detained for status offenses. And while between 1974 and 1979 admissions to juvenile correctional institutions declined by only 2.9 percent, to 65,416, this low rate masks a much more precipitous decline of 37 percent in female admissions (Krisberg and Schwartz 1983:342–44). Again, this development probably reflects increased unwillingness to incarcerate status offenders. The resultant impact upon some programs was dramatic. Illinois, for example, had for several decades operated a state correctional institution for girls with a capacity of some 300. Throughout the 1960s, the institution constantly was threatened by overcrowding. Finally, authorization and money were made available for the construction of a new institution giving the state considerably increased capacity for the incarceration of juvenile girls. The building was constructed but never opened for its originally intended use. Before it was completed, the state had passed legislation creating the status offender category and forbidding the incarceration of its members in institutions for delinquents. Most juvenile female inmates had been committed for running away, truancy, sex offense, or being ungovernable—all status offenses. Within a comparatively short time, the state had only some 20 girls in correctional institutional care. Not only was the new institution not opened—the old one was soon closed. The small population of juvenile girl "incarcerees" was moved to a coed institution.

For some years, then, progress toward the deinstitutionalization of status offenders seems to have been made (though the data do not permit definitive answers to questions as to what proportion of those "deinstitutionalized" are actually in private or mental health rather than public correctional institutions). The degree to which any actual progress toward the goal of deinstitutionalization can be maintained or expanded probably depends to a considerable extent, in turn, on the degree to which movement takes place toward the provision of resources for diversion to alternative, community-based services and programs. As we have noted, the expansion of the use of diversion to alternative programs has proved a much more complicated task than had earlier been envisioned.

Divestment

The final, hotly debated proposal for limiting the role of authoritative state intervention calls for the removal of status offenders from the jurisdiction of the juvenile court and justice system. Such a step is often referred to as "decriminalization." That term seems to us to be confusing and inaccurate. In most states, juvenile court law defines as non-criminal all actions regarding juvenile offenders taken by or authorized by the juvenile court. Thus we here follow Kobrin and Klein's (1983) suggestion that what is actually sought is the divestment from the justice system of its central, controlling role in the confrontation between society and the status offender.

However termed, we come to the conclusion that the juvenile court's role with respect to the status offender should be that of a resource to be employed only rarely, in carefully and narrowly defined circumstances, and then only after all reasonable efforts to arrive at solutions through voluntary structures have proven unsuccessful. We come to this conclusion with some reluctance. We are quite aware that authoritarian intervention into the life of the child is sometimes necessary and beneficial. We are aware that some youngsters will go unaided who might have been helped if coercive intervention remained readily possible. We are concerned lest the retention of jurisdiction only over truly delinquent youths heighten the stigmatization inherent in the justice system process. We should regret further loss of the public's perception of the court and justice system as a source of help as well as punishment. But we also believe that, very generally, if effective help can be given to the child and family in which communication and control have broken down, it can most often be given by voluntary services. We further believe that assignment to the justice system of priority in the service delivery role does tend to absolve from responsibility the family, the school, the social agency, and other structures that must ultimately move toward the solution of difficulties in child-family-community relationships. And we are keenly aware of the dangers of abuse or unwise use of authority inherent in the justice system's status offender jurisdiction. After all, it has been not entirely as a result of benevolence that some thousands of status offenders have in recent years found themselves incarcerated in correctional institutions.

While we favor termination of the juvenile court's broad jurisdiction over status offenders, we are aware that some provision must be made for carefully restricted intervention in the lives of youngsters whose behaviors place them in substantial and immediate danger. The design of such provision, without creating the proverbial "camel with its nose under the tent" pathway to abuse is difficult. We would anticipate that in the near future various jurisdictions will explore differing paths to this end. It seems probable to us that such pathways may often resemble those suggested by the Institute of Judicial Administration, American Bar Association Juvenile Justice Standards Project's volume on non-criminal misbehavior (IJA-ABA 1977).

The IJA-ABA's proposals have been fairly closely followed in the recent (1982) revision by Illinois of its Juvenile Court Act. Under them, law enforcement officers determining that a juvenile is in circumstances constituting substantial and immediate danger to the juvenile's physical safety may take the juvenile into "limited custody" for a period not to exceed six hours. During that time, efforts should be made to release the juvenile to parents or guardians. If this proves impossible, or if the juvenile or guardian refuses release, or if the subject is a runaway refusing to return home, the juvenile is taken to a "temporary nonsecure residential facility licensed by the state for such purpose." If by the end of 21 days' care in the facility, it remains impossible to release the juvenile to his home, a neglect petition may be filed in his behalf, though if the parent and child agree in writing, the period of stay in the facility could be extended beyond 21 days. No further placement could be made without agreement of both the juvenile and the parents or guardian, except by court order resulting from the filing of a neglect petition. Placement in a secure detention facility or institution for the treatment of juveniles accused of crime or adjudged delinquent would be permitted in no event.

Proposals such as those made by the IJA would necessitate the development of a broad spectrum of pertinent voluntary child welfare services: crisis intervention programs, walk-in shelters, "hot lines," and others. But we are convinced of the validity of the institute's analysis of the next steps currently necessary to discharge the societal responsibility for the troubled and therefore troublesome child in our midst: "Many years ago, the British legal historian, Sir Henry Maine, wrote that the progress of civilized society was marked by the transition from status to contract. . . . It is time that American society took that transitional step in its response to family-based problems centered on the noncriminal misbehavior of children. By relying on noncoerced and extrajudicial services rather than court-imposed sanctions in status offense cases, these standards attempt to provide a basis for that step" (IJA-ABA 1977:21.)

CHAPTER 6

THE DISPOSITIONAL EXTREMES: DIVERSION AND THE CORRECTIONAL INSTITUTION

If one accepts our guidelines for disposition, including adherence to the least restrictive feasible alternative, there is little doubt that the majority of juvenile offenders will be cared for by the use of diversion in one form or another, and in noninstitutional settings. However, there is also little doubt that a diminished but still significant number will be referred to juvenile correctional institutions. Major social policy issues about each of these dispositional extremes are currently the subject of discourse more often characterized by impassioned reference to ideology than by the guidance of analysis of the lessons of experience. It is thus essential that we take stock of the major current issues about the design and implementation of each of these widely varying services for juvenile offenders.

The Diversion of Delinquency Cases

We are not utopian in our expectations concerning early development of resources for the diversion of delinquents from the justice system. That system always has and always will suffer from the malady of "resource starvation." The delinquent simply does not arouse sympathy or readiness to devise and support helping resources in the same way as does the physically ill child. Nonetheless, recent years *have* seen some progress. By fits and starts, a social policy climate nurturing the growth of often very imaginative programs has emerged. The continued existence of that climate will not only depend on its ideological basis, though the importance of that basis must not be underestimated. Also crucial to its vitality is thoughtful analysis of the very real problems emerging from the practice of diversion in recent years. We would suggest that attention be focused on four critical points at which disposition decisions must be made: at the time of the youth's initial encounter with police; at detention intake; at court intake; and at court adjudication. The police, for example, have a variety of options available to them. They may merely sharply reprimand misbehaving youths and send them on their way, with the hope that some slight intimidation will discourage them from further mischief. A ride around the block in a squad car or a visit to the local precinct may serve a similar purpose. For some youths, however, more strenuous options must be exercised including referral to a wide range of diversion programs (such as crisis intervention, family counseling, employment counseling, tutoring, or residential placement). For some, referral to juvenile court is inevitable.

Youths who are considered dangerous to themselves or others, or who are considered to be runaway risks, may also be taken to a local detention center or jail to await a court hearing. A wide range of options exists at this point as well, to be exercised by the individual who has responsibility for overseeing detention intake decisions. For example, youths may be placed in secure detention, in home, foster, or group home detention, or may simply be released on their own recognizance to await their day in court. A similar range of options exists for those responsible for court intake and for judges who preside at juvenile court hearings. At the point of either court intake or the adjudication hearing, youths may be referred to a residential diversion program—a group home, independent living program, psychiatric placement, for instance—or to a nonresidential diversion program, such as vocational training, restitution, or dispute mediation. Of course, at adjudication judges also have the option of committing juveniles to a state training school.

As we noted earlier, the emphasis on the use of noninstitutional placements began in earnest during the 1960s, at about the time of the appointment of President Johnson's Commission on Law Enforcement and Administration of Justice. In many respects, the juvenile justice field has benefited from the spate of noninstitutional programs that has emerged since that time, especially from the effort that has been devoted to the design and implementation of humane services for juveniles. Countless youths have avoided unnecessary incarceration and have received useful services as a result of these efforts. Yet, as we have also noted, the trend toward diversion and deinstitutionalization has borne hearty and frequently deserved criticism. Clearly, this movement has experienced growing pains, some of which have undermined efforts to proliferate the programs.

The principal difficulties that noninstitutional programs have encountered generally involve policies governing intake and the design and delivery of services. With respect to intake, for example, there is considerable evidence that factors unrelated to the seriousness of a juvenile's offense or the danger he represents frequently determine whether a youth is handled formally or informally by police and court personnel. Thus, extralegal factors such as gender and race have been shown in some jurisdictions to be strong predictors of the offense with which a juvenile is charged and the likelihood that he or she will be placed in secure detention. Officials who are concerned about the need to protect females from sexual exploitation, for instance, are sometimes more likely to charge females than males as status offenders in order to render them eligible for residential placements and "get them off of the streets." In some communities, race may affect the severity of the charge filed. The persistence with which community-based alternatives are pursued may also depend upon the local flavor of race relations, the personal biases of arresting officers, and similar extralegal factors. Regrettably, there is evidence that in many jurisdictions the strongest predictor of the likelihood that a youth will be placed in secure detention is the number of beds available; jurisdictions that have a greater detention capacity tend to detain at a higher rate.

Although the influence of extralegal factors varies considerably from locale to locale, the accumulated evidence is clear. In too many instances the demographic traits of a juvenile, or local administrative or political idiosyncrasies, have greater influence on the way in which juvenile offenders are handled than do the nature of the offense and the genuine risk the youths represent to themselves and others. As a consequence, many noninstitutional programs and institutional facilities have been saddled with youths who have been misplaced and for whom appropriate services and supervision may not exist.

Similar problems result from the phenomena of net-widening and rela-beling. Net-widening occurs when the creation of a program or a set of services leads to the expansion of control over the lives of youths who otherwise would have been ignored or handled less intrusively. There is evidence that net-widening has emerged as a prominent unintended and frequently expensive by-product of noninstitutional services. Consistent with the adage that supply affects demand, there has been a predictable tendency in recent years for the inauguration of noninstitutional services to result in larger numbers of youths and youths with substantially less serious offense histories being brought under the purview of the juvenile court. Granted, not all professionals regard this as a deleterious outcome. Some argue that net-widening has increased the likelihood that youths in need of services will have access to them; the additional sections woven into the net are a boon to youths, not a restraint. Critics argue, though, that the benefits of these services have yet to be proven and that until they are the broadening of juvenile justice represents gratuitous social control. Austin and Krisberg (1981:188–89) have argued, for example, that " 'widening the net' describes the nightmare of the benevolent state gone haywire. This horror has already been vividly portrayed in Orwell's *1984*, Solzhenitsyn's *Cancer Ward*, Kesey's *One Flew Over the Cuckoo's Nest*, and Burgess' *Clockwork Orange*. Social scientists and criminolo-gists have just caught up with the humanists."

A problem closely tied to net-widening is that of relabeling. Relabel-ing typically occurs when a particular set of services is limited to a particular group of clients, so that access to the services by others is restricted. Thus, in jurisdictions where certain counseling services are earmarked for status offenders, youths who previously would have been referred to the state department of social services as dependent or ne-glected children may be referred to the juvenile court to qualify them for services designated for "minors in need of supervision." Or if local policy is altered to prohibit secure detention for status offenders—as happened in hundreds of jurisdictions following the enactment of the 1974 Juvenile Justice and Delinquency Prevention Act—youths who previously would have been charged as status offenders may be charged with a delinquent offense in order to satisfy the intake criteria of the local detention center. As a consequence of such relabeling, both nonin-stitutional and secure detention facilities have been forced to arrange services and care for youths who have not traditionally been their responsibility. Again, this is not to say that relabeling is necessarily detrimental; it is important to acknowledge, however, that inappropriate referrals at least raise serious questions of due process.

The central due process issue stems from the lack of judicial oversight that frequently accompanies decisions to detain, release, or divert. Questions of due process are especially troublesome when decisions are made at the time of youths' encounters with police, when officers' substantial discretion may escape judicial monitoring entirely. Thus, police decisions to release or detain, and decisions about whether a youth should be charged as a minor in need of supervision, delinquent, or whatever, are often truly autonomous and subject to no review. Though there is no reason to assume that police necessarily misuse their discretion, one cannot ignore the volumes of evidence that demonstrate that extralegal factors frequently determine the disposition of a youth's encounter with the police, factors which, in principle, should have no bearing on the officer's decision.

One of the greatest due process dangers is that a youth may be subjected to subtle coercion at the time of encounter with the police. The police may in effect function as both judge and jury when they offer youths an ultimatum: either accept an offer of referral to a diversion program (counseling, restitution, etc.), or take a ride to the precinct. Critics frequently allege that such choices are often forced, so that on occasion a truly innocent youth who is fearful or who would have some difficulty establishing his defense may reluctantly accept the officer's "conviction" as the path of least resistance.

Similar problems can arise at the next stage in the process, referral to court. Services that have been designed as court diversion programs are often assigned before any formal adjudication hearing. Fortunately, because decisions made at the time of court intake are made in a judicial setting by personnel affiliated with the court, they are ordinarily subjected to greater scrutiny than are decisions made by the police. Though administrative decisions can also lead to mislabeling, the odds are diminished.

The due process dilemma tends to be less severe once one moves beyond the points of encounter with police and court intake officials. Detention decisions, for example, are ordinarily reviewed by a juvenile court judge or referee, if not immediately then within hours of the youth's admission to the detention facility or jail. Similarly, decisions to divert following the adjudication hearing benefit from judicial review. Problems can arise, however, in jurisdictions where court administrative personnel make diversion decisions between the time of court intake and the adjudication hearing, without judicial review.

Another thorn in the side of many well-intentioned diversion programs has been the phenomenon of "creaming"—the tendency for some programs to restrict admission to youths with less rather than more severe offense histories. Several factors give rise to creaming. Police and court officials, for example, sometimes are reluctant to refer to diversion or alternative-to-detention programs youths who have been charged with a serious offense or who possess substantial offense histories. The risk seems too great, both for the safety of the community and for the reputation of law enforcement officials who would be criticized should the youths misbehave. Staff of the diversion programs themselves also may cream, for somewhat different reasons. A well-known fact of life in most diversion programs is that continued funding may depend on the program's track record. Programs that limit the number of serious offenders admitted may increase their "success" rate. In addition, youths with deep-seated problems tend to require more staff and better-trained staff than youths with less serious problems. To the extent that problem-laden youths are more expensive to serve, programs that operate on a fixed budget may lean toward "light" juvenile offenders. A practical consequence of creaming is that youths who are most in need of services may not be referred to them. This phenomenon may also exacerbate the problem of net-widening, to the extent that programs fill their caseloads with youths who would have been ignored otherwise or supervised in a less ambitious fashion.

The Problem of Labels

Much of the popular rhetoric about the goals of deinstitutionalization and diversion is based on an assumption that juvenile offenders can and should be categorized as, for example, status offenders, delinquents, serious offenders, and so on. Legislation frequently makes explicit reference to these groups in an effort to mandate or earmark services. Unfortunately, there is considerable evidence that "pure" groups do not in fact exist, except, perhaps, in our imagination. In one study of a statewide program designed to provide alternatives to detention for status offenders, for example, it was found that the majority of youths (57 percent) admitted to the program on the basis of one status offense charge had histories that included delinquent and/or violent offenses as well; only slightly more than one-fourth of these youths had offense histories comprised primarily of status offenses (Spergel et al. 1981). Similar results, indicating that there are relatively few pure status or delinquent offenders, were obtained by Erickson (1979) in his comprehensive survey of both self-report and official arrest data for several cohorts of youths. In fact, only 8 percent of the youths referred to the Pima County, Arizona deinstitutionalization of status offender projects were pure status offenders. These findings are not atypical, and suggest that restricting or requiring services for youths on the basis of offender categories may rest on a false assumption that any offense with which a youth is charged provides a useful indication of the seriousness of his offense career. Regrettably, it is not unusual to find a youth who has a disconcertingly long history of delinquent offenses admitted to a nonsecure program for status offenders because of one recently committed status offense. The nominal label attached to a police report frequently does not provide an accurate description of the youths with whom we deal.

The vagueness of labels has created confusion in other respects. The 1974 Juvenile Justice and Delinquency Prevention Act clearly was drafted, in part, to encourage a reduction in the numbers of youths incarcerated in state training schools and other secure correction or detention facilities. That goal was foreshadowed by the 1967 report of the President's Commission on Law Enforcement and Administration of Justice. And for some years now, a noteworthy decline has appeared in the numbers of institutionalized youths, at least in data on the annual census of youths in custody. Yet a perceptive analysis by Lerman (1980) suggests that this impression is misguided and in large part due to the slippery nature of official labels. In particular, it seems that while in recent years there has been a decline in the numbers of youths held in public correctional institutions, the numbers of delinquent youths in institutions for children generally have not declined. Many juvenile offenders have been relabeled in a way that renders them eligible for admission to a private child care institution that specializes in "problem," "disturbed," or "acting out" youths. Thus, many juveniles who previously would have been placed in a public correctional facility have been relabeled and referred to other institutions, rather than being placed in nonsecure community-based facilities. The widespread availability during the 1970s of Title XX and other federal funds for subsidizing out-of-home care of juveniles served to encourage this shuffling. What appeared at first blush to be a precipitous decline in the population of institutionalized juvenile offenders was in large part illusory. Though there is no reason to conclude that these decisions represent a conspiracy on the part of child welfare workers to sidestep the goals of the U.S. Congress and the Office of Juvenile Justice and Delinquency Prevention with respect to deinstitutionalization, there is some support for the cynic's view that some of this relabeling was motivated by organizational self-interest. In some cases, it appears, youths have been relabeled as a way to ensure that they remain in secure custody; if they can't be held under the auspices of the local corrections agency, some other bureaucratic home will be found. In other instances, it seems that private agencies have encouraged relabeling to ensure referrals to their facilities, especially in those that were experiencing a decline in referrals from other sources. In all fairness, a considerable portion of relabeling has been a relatively innocent by-product of the transfer of legal responsibility for certain juveniles (particularly status offenders) from the juvenile court to public child welfare or social service agencies, whose personnel may have a tendency to view mischievous youths as candidates for social rather than correctional services. Nonetheless, relabeling has occurred and has contributed to inaccurate assumptions about the extent to which the goals of deinstitutionalization have been met.

It should be clear, however, that despite difficulties, enormous numbers of youths have been diverted from formal processing by the police, juvenile court, and secure correctional facilities. Hundreds of thoughtful programs have been devised by scores of conscientious professionals, directed ultimately toward the effective treatment of juvenile offenders and a reduction of disturbingly high recidivism rates. But despite these efforts, the critics have been out in force ever since the first diversion program was conceived, with indictments of everything from the physical location of community-based programs to the quality of their staffs. The denunciation of diversion has become a sociological fashion in recent years. Catchwords such as "widening the net," "stigmatization," and "labeling" serve as a sort of shorthand that expresses real problems, but, as Binder and Geis (1984) rather vehemently note, may also serve as alternatives to objective examination. The debates between critics and proponents have been rich—though not always polite—and once the smoke clears, they provide a great many lessons about what has gone well or ill with a major contemporary social movement.

Problems of Implementation

The most persistent issues tend to concern a series of unanticipated consequences related to the cost and design of so-called community-based programs and the services that typically accompany them. Some of the more vigorous controversies have centered on myths concerning the expenses involved in implementing these programs. For years in most jurisdictions the premise has circulated that one of the principal virtues of diversion and deinstitutionalization programs is that they are far less costly to administer. According to popular rhetoric it is patently obvious that programs that divert youths from the expensive bureaucracies of police and juvenile court, and from 24-hour institutions, save money; after all, community-based programs tend to have fewer staff, require the maintenance of less costly physical plants, and can adapt more quickly to the unpredictable forces of supply and demand than can the traditional public correctional facilities bound by rigid civil service guidelines or union contracts. Community-based programs, it has been argued, are simply more cost effective on many counts, especially those that contract for services on an as-needed basis, rather than hire permanent, year-round staff.

In recent years, however, evidence has emerged that indicates quite consistently that prevailing assumptions are misleading. For a variety of complex reasons, it now appears that a large number—though certainly not all—of alternative programs are at least as costly if not more so than traditional ways of handling juvenile offenders. We referred to one of the main culprits earlier—the phenomenon of net-widening. It stands to reason that jurisdictions that are sweeping more youths into their systems as a result of the creation of new community-based programs, without a commensurate decline in the numbers of youths handled in the traditional fashion, are increasing their aggregate costs, though the average cost per youth may be lower. Group homes and foster care ordinarily are cheaper than bricks-and-mortar institutions, but in the long run savings will not be realized if the flow of youths processed through the juvenile justice system is heavier following the introduction of alternative programs. A typical finding is that of Bohnstedt (1978), who found in his study of eleven diversion projects in California that while it was approximately $320 less expensive per client to serve youths under the auspices of diversion programs rather than traditional probation, no net savings were realized; nearly half of the cases served by the eleven projects normally would not have been served by the courts at all.

But increased costs can also result for other reasons. In some jurisdictions, though the net has not been widened, youths referred to community-based programs spend, on the average, longer periods of time under supervision than they would have had they been handled in more traditional ways. The motive may be noble—to provide these youths with services that they apparently need—yet the consequence of increased costs can be burdensome. In his study of community treatment in California, Lerman (1975) found that juveniles placed in community-based programs had their periods of treatment extended from 8 to about 36 months. As Hylton (1982:368–69) has noted, "It is increasingly apparent that commitment to community-based programs usually entails longer periods under supervision than does commitment to traditional prisons and training schools."

Unfortunately, despite the frequently admirable intentions of many program staff, it is clear that in some instances the length of stay is extended for less acceptable reasons. It is no secret that the availability of enormous sums for community-based programs has attracted a fair number of opportunistic entrepreneurs along with the majority of well-meaning, conscientious professionals who are committed to helping troubled youths. The manner in which many alternative programs have been funded—a per diem fee paid for each youth served—may well provide incentives to extend periods of service. Few public agencies have developed strategies for dealing adequately with this dilemma, most likely because there is no simple solution. If one reduces the per diem, the quality of service may drop commensurately and talented service providers may be discouraged from participating. Similarly, if agencies are paid an annual prepaid "retainer," unaffected by the daily census, sufficient incentives may not exist to admit the youths who genuinely need service or to provide quality services to those accepted.

Further, in some instances, funding arrangements have encouraged the purchase of more rather than less expensive services. For example, when the Illinois Department of Children and Family Services planned its participation in the federal Deinstitutionalization of Status Offenders program in the mid-1970s, it estimated that only 20 percent of youths arrested by the police would need an out-of-home placement, for example, foster or group home care; it was expected that the rest of the youths participating in the alternative-to-detention program would be supervised adequately in their own homes by staff of local social service agencies with which the state contracted. As the program unfolded, a number of service providers brought considerable pressure to bear to increase the use of the more expensive out-of-home placements. As the evaluators of this program observed: "Pressures by the nonprofit and private agencies led [program staff] to revise its estimate of the proportion of youths who would need out-of-home placement; the rate was increased from 20 to 40 percent. In fact, after a year and one-half of program operations, about 65 percent of all youths were in placement the first night" (Spergel et al. 1982:439).

Unexpected costs associated with community-based programs also come from more subtle sources, and therefore are often overlooked by evaluators. Analyses that examine the costs and benefits of these programs frequently compare the expenses involved in administering community-based services with those of institutionalized care, that is, staff salaries, purchase of services, building maintenance, insurance premiums, supplies. Rarely do such analyses take into account costs incurred by the general community as a result of the development of diversion and deinstitutionalization programs. For example, as we noted earlier, youths referred to community-based programs tend, on the average, to have recidivism rates comparable to those of institutionalized youths, though exceptions do exist. What this means is that the communities that sponsor community-based programs expend considerable effort and money when these youths commit new offenses while participating in the programs. Expenses are incurred for police protection and investigation, related security costs, court costs, property damage, disability claims and medical care, insurance claims, and so on (Hylton 1982:365). A careful accounting of these costs may reveal that community-based programs are not the bargain many of us have assumed them to be.

The cost of providing community-based care also depends to a considerable degree on the nature and extent of services provided to youths referred to them. Some are simply more expensive than others. Placement in a group home, where one pays for 24-hour supervision, meals, and a physical facility, will usually cost more than in-home supervision, whose principal costs include staff time and benefits, telephone fees, and gasoline. Vocational training programs that provide hands-on experience with equipment typically are more costly than restitution or counseling programs.

The Assignment of Services

Regrettably, there is little consensus about the nature of services that ought to be provided to misbehaving youths, and little evidence that a strong correlation exists between the nature of services provided and improved status, measured in whatever way (social functioning, self-esteem, recidivism). What services ultimately are provided tend to depend somewhat idiosyncratically on a variety of factors, among them the size of a program's budget, the availability of service providers in the local area, the professional preferences of program staff (for example, whether they are inclined toward residential or nonresidential care, counseling or concrete services), and the financial or political incentives to provide specific services. Geography too can make a difference. In the Illinois program youths in the large, urban section of the state (Chicago/Cook County) were much more likely to receive an out-of-home placement than were youths in a more rural region in the mid-section of the state, even after controlling for a variety of individual differences among youths in the program. Also, females and black youths were more likely to be placed in foster care; males were more likely to be given counseling and white youths were more likely to be placed in a shelter or group home facility. Younger youths tended to be placed out-of-home, while older youths more frequently were permitted to remain in their own homes. It is difficult to account for these trends; possible causes range from institutional racism to paternalism. Nevertheless, it is evident that the nature and extent of services

provided to juvenile offenders referred to diversion and deinstitutionalization programs often are not a function of rational deliberations
about each juvenile's individual needs and the right communities have
to protect themselves; the factors of race, age, gender, cost, and geography apparently account for a significant portion of the variance.

Whether services are provided under public or private auspices can also
have a dramatic effect on who gets served and how. In recent years there
has been a noteworthy attempt in many jurisdictions to increase the
number of services provided youthful offenders by the private sector
rather than public agencies. In many communities, juvenile courts or
departments of corrections contract with private social service agencies—
some nonprofit and some proprietary—to provide, for example, foster or
group home care, counseling, vocational training, or in-home supervision.
This increased use of private agencies reflects both an ideological commitment in some quarters that the private rather than the public sector should
provide for the needs of citizens whenever possible and an attempt to trim
the budgets of public agencies. A widespread though not always well-sup-
ported assumption among professionals is that services frequently can be
delivered more competently and efficiently by private agencies that have
incentives to pinch the public's pennies in order to be competitive finan-
cially, and are not burdened by the limitations and complexities of the civil
service system. Private agencies, it is assumed, can do much of what they
please, and have the ability to hire and lay off employees in response to
sporadic downturns and upturns in the economy and in the pace of
referrals to the programs. It is also commonly argued that the atmosphere
that surrounds private programs fosters a level of creativity and enthusiasm that public programs find hard to match; the absence of state-issue
paint, furniture, clothing, cinder-block construction, and personnel codes
can do wonders for morale. In the end, youths benefit from the availability
of services that are of superior quality and administered efficiently.

But how safe are these assumptions? Not surprisingly, it turns out
that the distinctions between publicly and privately administered services are not so clear. For one thing, as we have suggested, privately run
community-based programs are not necessarily less expensive than conventional programs operated under public auspices. If the net is widened, lower per diems mean relatively little: 100 (youths) $\times$ $40/day is
more than 75 (youths) $\times$ $50/day. The burdens of increased community
surveillance and related obligations also tend to drive up the costs.

So how do we respond to the critic who argues that competition among private agencies for a slice of the government pie will tend to keep a lid on costs, just as the classical economists predict? Well, in some instances the invisible hand of free enterprise may foster that result. However, there is still the old adage to contend with, "You get what you pay for." There is some appeal in contracting with private agencies on the basis of competitive proposals, but state standard-setting and vigorous program monitoring are necessary to ensure that funded programs are not lean in quality as well as budget.

Studies have also shown that in a discouragingly large number of community-based programs services that are earmarked for juvenile offenders never quite make it to them. This appears to be due in part to our tendency to place greater emphasis on efforts to remove youths from institutions than to design streamlined methods for delivering community-based care. Also, program staff and related personnel often have caseloads so large that there is little opportunity to provide meaningful time to their charges. This is nothing new, of course. The 1967 President's Commission on Law Enforcement and Administration of Justice made the same observation. What seems new is the number of juveniles who never appear at the community-based programs to which they have been referred. Dunford's (1977:338) review of the outcome of a police diversion program provides a warning of a possible danger: "Of the 106 diverted young people, 41 (38%) received no services. . . . Of this number 48 percent were unknown to the alleged receiving agency and 14 percent refused service. The remaining 38 percent were on the records of the diversion project as having been received and as having been assessed for youth needs, but not as receiving services. Project personnel could not explain the loss. These youths had 'fallen through the cracks.' "

The Use of Coercion

In too many instances, those youths who do show up for services do so under the threat of coercion, rather than because there is a genuine desire on the part of both youth and staff to pursue constructive solutions to the juveniles' difficulties. The arguments for and against coerced treatment are straightforward. On the one hand, if youths are going to be deterred from future mischief, they must be shown that juvenile justice agencies have teeth. If apprehended youths are simply referred to community-based programs without the requirement of participation—and without penalties for failing to participate successfully—it would not take long for word to spread that the police and courts are not taking juvenile misbehavior seriously.

Critics allege, however, that coercion and effective treatment simply don't mix, and real solutions to youths' problems depend on their willingness to participate voluntarily in programs designed to provide them with insight into their difficulties, marketable skills, wholesome environment, and similar benefits. The difficult reality may be that one can expect little in the way of favorable results if intended beneficiaries are not motivated to participate in services made available to them.

Both points of view have merit. Juveniles do tend to be "savvy." They can often see through empty threats. Referral to a service program without ability to require participation will often lead to nonappearance or to half-hearted involvement. For example, in his evaluation of the effort to implement the voluntary deinstitutionalization of status offenders project in Pima County, Arizona, Erickson (1979) found that only 30 percent of the cases recommended for treatment actually found their way to programs to which they were referred. In addition, it was found that a large proportion of those who did show up appeared only once and came from one of the referral agencies that provided transportation to the recommended facilities the first time. When transportation was discontinued, those who did show up constituted only 17 percent of those recommended for services. As Erickson observed: "It is unlikely that this is a transportation problem. Instead it reflects the absence of a legal threat and perceived need for therapy. Therefore, all things considered, it is difficult to be optimistic about the success of the 'hands-off' approach in solving the problems it has set out to solve."

Neither the origins of nor a fully satisfactory solution to the problems experienced by the Pima County and other projects is readily evident. We do not know the extent to which local juvenile justice decision makers employed referral simply out of felt need to do something, rather than as a result of sophisticated analysis leading to conviction that a particular service was appropriate for a particular youngster. Nor do we know the extent to which agency personnel were equipped to perform one of the most demanding roles in the helping services: skillfully and with depth of commitment reaching out to people in trouble, helping them appreciate the realities of their situations, the alternatives available to them and the probable consequence of adopting each, the nature of helping services available, and the necessary elements of their own meaningful use of such services. Effective case referral and program intake are functions often taken for granted but actually demanding the very finest in professional know-how and in personal aptitude.

There remain obdurate issues beyond the necessity for skill and dedication. Definitive guidelines spelling out the situations under which coercion may be necessary and justified are not available. Their development is a pressing need. Thus, we should like to make some contribution to the dialogue.

It seems clear to us that certain types of justice system disposition of juvenile cases must remain legally enforceable. This is obviously true in situations in which the necessity is *incapacitation* as a means of societal protection. The goal may involve commitment to secure care, but it may also involve such community dispositions as those providing close surveillance, residence in open but still somewhat restricted settings, required regular attendance at work, or observation of a curfew. The power to enforce would also appear to be a natural and normal accompaniment of an order meant to assure some form of *restitution*. As we noted earlier, such orders may provide for direct restitution to victims or for some form of symbolic restitution, as in the requirement to engage in prescribed community service. We assume, though not with certainty, that an argument can be made for the power to enforce in another much more shadowy group of cases arising from situations in which the effort is to *reinforce the authority of concerned and capable parents.* We also assume that orders *requiring behaviors expected of all youths,* such as to attend school up to a legally prescribed age, should be considered enforceable.

We are much more dubious of state power to enforce participation in counseling, psychotherapy, group activity, or other remedial programs, attendance at which is ordered as a consequence of offender status and is designed to treat presumed mental or emotional disorders, enhance socialization, expedite youths' maturation, alter their self-concepts, or in other ways engage with their psyches. We are quite aware of the enormous contribution to health, happiness, and productive citizenship frequently arising from participation in such endeavors. We are also convinced that in some cases, the benefits may be derived from enforced participation. But as we have previously asserted, the outcomes of the various available forms of psychological treatment are unpredictable. They may be helpful, but it is not uncommon for them to prove harmful. Further, the authority to require participation in programs providing life experiences that can neither be precisely defined nor anticipated, and the outcomes of which cannot be accurately specified or measured, creates the danger of debasement of the therapeutic enterprise so as to cause it to become an exercise in the abuse of authority and the imposition of regimes born of frustrated anger. After all, we are not far in time from the use of "hydrotherapy" in the form of spread-eagling youths against brick walls by the power of high-pressure water hoses!

We thus return to our earlier prescription urging the responsibility of the state to provide imaginatively designed *opportunity* for growth and change but not to require participation. We are aware that some cases will be lost that might have benefited if coercion had been possible. But the possible loss of freedom, the invasion of privacy, the danger of psychological or other harm, and the possible debasement of treatment programs is too high a price to pay for the often-dubious benefits of enforced therapy. And, we further believe that quality programs of proven efficacy are most likely to emerge in situations in which they must enlist voluntary participation. Competition resulting from a healthy measure of consumer choice is probably just as productive of quality products in this as in other fields of endeavor.

What Is "Community-Based" Care?

Debate around the coercive character of noninstitutional services to juvenile offenders is rendered more acrimonious by the absence of consensus on what "community-based" means. Some of these programs have been organized around a particular service approach (for example, restitution, wilderness/adventure programs), and some have been designed to serve particular subgroups of juvenile offenders (for example, runaways, serious offenders). Some of them operate essentially without locks, keys, and other mechanical restraints, and others—especially those designed for violent offenders—operate under strict security. Some place considerable emphasis on promoting contact between residents and family or other community people, while others do not. In the haste to develop noninstitutional programs—especially following the passage of the 1974 Juvenile Justice and Delinquency Prevention Act—programs of every shape and size have emerged, with striking variation in characteristics such as treatment approach, staffing patterns, services, admission and discharge criteria, length of stay, and size. As a result of this diversity, the term "community-based" has been used for programs ranging from highly secure, nonvoluntary group homes for violent offenders to nonresidential, voluntary vocational training. In short, "community-based" has come to refer to nearly any program operated outside a traditional correctional facility, that is, a synonym for noninstitutional. A practical consequence of this ambiguity is that programs of widely ranging quality have been dubbed community-based and thus qualified for government funds earmarked for this general purpose.

The lack of precision in legislative acts and administrative guidelines has also contributed to the wide variation in the character and quality of noninstitutional programs. For example, the 1974 Juvenile Justice and Delinquency Prevention Act specified only that

> the term "community-based" facility, program or service means a small, open group home or other suitable place located near the juvenile's home or family and programs of community supervision and service which maintain community and consumer participation in the planning, operation, and evaluation of their programs which may include, but are not limited to, medical, educational, vocational, social, and psychological guidance, training, counseling, alcoholism treatment, drug treatment, and other rehabilitative services.

This legislation provided little guidance to and few limitations on those who sought to develop noninstitutional programs. No mention was made of the nature and frequency of contacts youths should have with community residents and agencies, or the nature and degree of security, supervision, or coercion that are appropriate or permissible. Community-based programs presumably should seek to strengthen a youth's ties with his surrounding community, especially with family members, school, religious and cultural institutions, and—where appropriate—employers. Yet the vagueness of guidelines has permitted many programs to flourish that do little to meet these basic goals.

An item that should therefore be placed prominently on the agenda of juvenile justice professionals is the refinement of the concept of community-based care. Noninstitutional programs for a large portion of juveniles processed by the police and court are more than a passing fad; they are here to stay—though their numbers may wax and wane over time—and it is important for us to place as much emphasis on the design of community-based programs as on the goal of removing juveniles from institutions. Programs located in a community setting are not necessarily programs of admirable quality. Noninstitutional programs are not necessarily better than institutional ones simply by virtue of their location, lack of fences, nonuniformed staff, and absence of cells; some are even more destructive. As Coates et al. (1978:12) observed following their evaluation of community-based and institutional programs in Massachusetts, "The term institution in correctional parlance calls up images of prison buildings isolated by distance or high walls from the surrounding community. As the community-based movement has progressed, many people have realized that even such facilities as group homes can share with the old-walled institutions an isolation that, it turns out, does not necessarily depend upon physical barriers."

Recent years, then, have taught that community-based programs, if they are truly to be such, must incorporate more than mere location outside an institution. Close attention must be paid as well to both the atmosphere within the program and the extent to which quality relationships are established with local agencies and community residents. Unfortunately, failure to adequately cultivate community support has undermined many an attempt to place juveniles into community-based programs. Paradoxically, some of the most secure programs for juveniles are those that began as nonsecure community-based alternatives but, because of objections, fears, and complaints voiced by neighborhood residents, eventually devised extensive security precautions and intensive supervision. Cohen (1979:343) has put it succinctly: "Deep-end projects—those that are genuine alternatives to incarceration—have to make a trade-off between treatment goals (which favour the integrated community setting) and security goals which favour isolation. The trade-off under these conditions will tend to favour security—resulting in programs which simulate or mimic the very features of the institution they set out to replace." Programs for so-called serious offenders are especially vulnerable to this problem, given the fear these youths frequently inspire.

There will continue, then, to be a relatively small percentage of juvenile offenders whose threat is so great that they cannot be cared for in open settings. Thus a major task for today's correctional policymakers is the reexamination of the residual role of institutional settings and the necessary standards of care to be provided by them. With the emphasis on diversion and community-based services, the subjects of institutional care and the quality of institutional life have been neglected.

The Remaining Role of the Juvenile Correctional Institution

The reforms and counterreforms sweeping juvenile corrections since approximately the mid-1960s have emerged, for the greater part, from disillusionment with all too common institutional abuses. Fundamental to the liberal perspective—and to federal governmental policy as expressed for several years by the U.S. Office of Juvenile Justice and Delinquency Prevention—has been a sense of shock at the perversions of the rehabilitative ideal that had come to light in the practices of too many juvenile correctional institutions. Sordid stories of routine beatings, physical and psychological tortures, and sexual and other aggression revolted many observers of the correctional scene. Thoughtful works such as those by Bartollas et al. (1976) documented the manner in which at least some institutions originally planned as examples of behavioral change within an atmosphere of respect and dignity can drift into hostility and fear.

As we have previously noted, the deinstitutionalization movement has meaningfully affected many lives. In particular, fewer juvenile girls are now confined in correctional institutions than was the case before the reform wave of the 1960s and 1970s. But the degree to which this trend has affected the relatively serious rather than the status offender or the "garden variety" minor delinquent is doubtful. Certainly, the goal of deinstitutionalization of the more serious offender is not shared by that numerous and influential group of prosecutors, law enforcement officers, and alarmed citizens constituting the hard liners in contemporary corrections. The members of that group are very generally not particularly concerned with whether the correctional institution achieves a rehabilitative function. Or if they are concerned with rehabilitation, they expect that it can best be achieved by the application of deterrent punishment. Their major interests are in societal protection through incapacitation and general deterrence. And they do exert powerful influence upon public policy, as shown by recent increases in commitment rates, following an earlier decline. The annual rate of training school admissions per 100,000 youths age 10 to the upper age of juvenile court jurisdiction had been increasing until 1974, when it reached 228. By the end of that year the deinstitutionalization movement began its impact, and by 1979 the rate had decreased by 2.6 percent. However, in 1979 the pendulum began to swing back again. By 1982 the rate had increased again to 238, or 7.2 percent above the 1979 rate, the increase being entirely in male admissions, with female admissions slightly declining. Thus, in 1982 some 57,000 male and 8,000 female juveniles were admitted to juvenile training schools. On the average day during that same year, some 25,000 youths were so incarcerated (National Council on Crime and Delinquency 1984). A series of factors, including sometimes unduly harsh interpretations of the "just deserts" or "justice" philosophies, mandatory or presumptive sentencing, ready transfer to adult criminal jurisdiction, juvenile habitual offender laws, and similar emphases, has produced its results, for good or ill.

To us, the shifts in general support of training schools and other sanctioning devices seem to result from shifts in the relative weights of competing ideologies rather than from reliable data on the outcome of incarceration as a fundament of social policy. Earlier we expressed our doubts of both the morality and the utility of unquestioning adherence to either side of the controversy. Although we are not confident that we can settle the debate, we should like to attempt a series of propositions to guide it.

As a first proposition, we would argue that *social policy prescriptions based upon the presumed ability to accurately characterize "the American juvenile correctional institution" rest upon so inadequate a foundation as to render their credibility doubtful in the extreme.* Juvenile correctional institutions fall into no single pattern. Some are remnants of the dark ages of corrections and some represent thoughtful attempts to embody decency in human relationships. Within the individual institutions, some youngsters will find positive and some will find destructive life experiences—indeed, most will find elements of both. Blanket acceptance of "deinstitutionalization" ignores complex realities almost, though (here we must admit to our prejudice) not quite as much as does enthusiastic adherence to the adage, "lock 'em up."

The disutility of a unitary concept of the juvenile correctional institution has long been demonstrable. In a rather elegant research analysis, Street et al. (1966), for example, classified institutions into three major organizational models according to their differing goals and program emphases:

1. Obedience-conformity, emphasizing secure custody, the inculcation of respect for authority, and training in conformity;

2. Reeducation-development, relying upon training leading to changes in attitudes and values, acquisition of skills, development of new personal resources and new social behaviors; and

3. Treatment, aspiring to personality change through achievement of insights and understandings preparatory for community living.

Each model strongly tended to produce distinctive patterns of administrative definition of goals and methods, staff performance, and staff perceptions of inmates and of goals with respect to them. Further, the particular goal model resulted in differentially shaped inmate behaviors, self-perceptions, and perceptions of their relationships with others. Again, in the California Department of the Youth Authority's exemplary Youth Center Project, Jesness (1975) and his associates demonstrated that institutional orientation to differing treatment theories (behaviorism versus transactional analysis) resulted in differing inmate perceptions and behaviors, and in postinstitutional recidivism rates differing from those achieved by traditional institutions. In the authority's Fricot Ranch experiment, Jesness (1965) demonstrated the possible differing impacts of varying institutional size and resulting milieu.

It is not only true that institutions differ markedly from one another. It is also evident that different youths may find in the same institution widely varying experiences. Thus, for example, Palmer (1974) presents evidence strongly suggesting that while a majority of delinquent youths committed to correctional care may do better if immediately released to competent community supervision and service, at least one discernible type of delinquent (the "power oriented") may be expected to make a somewhat better community adjustment if first experiencing a period of good correctional institutional care.

In sum, then, "the juvenile correctional institution" is not a unitary concept. A sort of undifferentiated enthusiasm for deinstitutionalization as a goal in itself may have had some justification as a means of making sure that the horrors of life in some institutions were banished from juvenile justice practice. But the time when an undifferentiated approach could be justified may be coming to an end. True, we cannot justify sending the young delinquent to the institution where he may be assaulted in the basement on the day of his arrival. But neither can we justify sending him back to community life to assault again—or, for that matter, to the probability of being raped in a back alley, or being shot for either membership in or refusal to join a neighborhood gang. The need in the years immediately ahead is for dialogue based upon more certain knowledge about what sorts of institutional or community life experience should be sought for different sorts of youngsters, confronted by various life problems and posing different threats to the safety of their fellow citizens. Until such knowledge is available, compulsory "people-processing" and "people-changing" procedures, inside or outside the institution, will be difficult to justify as being in any sense rehabilitative.

As a second proposition, we would maintain that, *although correctional administrators and staff members, as well as legislators funding state departments of corrections, very generally assume that the institutions in question are engaged in a process of "correcting" their wards, they rarely take steps to determine the degree, if any, to which their efforts achieve any such consequence.* "Correction" is usually assumed by those functionaries involved to include ensuring that as a result of their correctional care wards will be disposed and enabled to live less crime-ridden lives upon their release than they would have lived had they remained "uncorrected." But institutional superintendents and their staff members characteristically are not provided with—and do not take steps to secure—information about the later careers of their wards. Anecdotally, some information may occasionally come their way. But systematic information, even upon wards' overall recidivism rates, much less upon broader measures of community adjustment, is rarely available. Attempts to determine which inmates, having been exposed to what regimes, later make what life adjustments are so rare as to be unknown to most practitioners.

The situation is not materially different concerning knowledge of the degree to which the shorter range goals within the institution are achieved. For example, institutions quite commonly announce their goals as including furthering academic achievement or vocational readiness. Often, they develop counseling or other programs calculated to enhance youths' positive self-concepts, concern for the rights of others, or other complex and sophisticated attitudinal changes. Instruments for measuring wards' positions with respect to those variables are fairly readily available. Sometimes, they are administered at the point of entry into the life of the institution and/or at the point of departure. Grotesquely, the information so generated is rarely aggregated and tabulated in such manner as to provide measures of the degree to which wards actually do or do not progress along hoped-for lines during the period of their institutionalization.

The prevailing absence of feedback upon inmates' within-institution progress or postinstitutional social behavior inhibits evaluation of correctional programs on the basis of outcome. Intuitive or vaguely impressionistic judgments are made, some of which may very well be correct. But, generally, administration, staff, and program units tend to be evaluated upon criteria having to do with whether general inmate conformity to the demands of institutional living seems to be produced. Inmate accommodation to such living is taken as the dominant measure of success. Serious questioning of the relevance of accommodation to subsequent community behavior is anxiety-provoking and is eschewed—despite the existence of a few studies which strongly suggest that little relationship exists between institutional and postinstitutional community adjustment.

We would further suggest that in large part as a result of the absence of feedback making rational evaluation possible, *juvenile correctional institution policy and methodology tend to result from a sense of policy vacuum, responses to competing charismas, and/or captivation by persuasively espoused fads that sweep the field in frequent succession.* Academic education, vocational training, a generally benign "institutional milieu therapy," psychiatrically oriented counseling and treatment, the promotion of intensive small-group experience through "Guided Group Interaction" or "Positive Peer Culture" programs, behavior modification through "token economies," treatment somehow related to "Interpersonal Maturity Level" diagnosis, and a variety of other approaches have all had their day. Each in its time has been hailed as the pathway to the future. Each has made valid contributions, but dedication to each has tended to be fleeting. The hard fact is that after some one hundred years' existence, the juvenile correctional institution has developed no tested and generally agreed-upon technology for the accomplishment of its complex and usually somewhat vaguely stated goals. In a weird sort of circularity, lack of pertinent technology both creates and is reinforced by a pervasive tendency for the institution to become an entity unto itself, apart from the broader community, inner-directed and concerned with the maintenance of its own equilibrium: a situation perhaps common to societal organizations but hardly conducive to maximum efficiency in preparing its participants for reentry into the broader world.

We do not pretend to be capable of advancing a panacea for these problems. To a large degree, we must fall back upon the standard prescription of the scholar: the adoption of the currently best available strategies for action is not enough; the additional responsibility of all engaged in the human services today is the supplementation of action strategies with strategies for knowledge development. When possible, such strategies must make use of research know-how and rigorous research design. But the problem is not always as complicated as it is made to seem. The first requisite is development of the information management systems necessary to sound administration in any field: systems that will assemble and aggregate the information that can feasibly be generated upon how many youth are served, of what sorts, for how long, how, by whom, at what cost, and with what outcome. An energetic beginning attack upon this problem should be possible to any imaginative administrator.

We have noted that at the present time no widely agreed-upon, empirically tested and verified technology for the accomplishment of change from a delinquency-oriented to a more productive way of life exists. But this conclusion must not be taken to mean that we cannot discern the major elements of an institutional life experience providing the impetus for eventual inmate personality growth and positive socialization. With deep concern we note that such elements are seldom clearly identified, verbalized, and promulgated as institutional goals against which policy and programs are measured. Until this is done, little progress can be made in identifying the "correctional" potential of the correctional institution. We thus attempt this task, doing so at a rather high level of abstraction. We believe it to be the responsibility of correctional practice everywhere to develop from such abstraction the behavioral specifics relevant to a given setting. We would thus suggest that the quality of the life experience provided the inmate of the juvenile correctional institution must be assessed in terms of the degree to which the following elements are present:

1. *Security,* or safety from physical threat. The societal purpose in committing youths to correctional care may include their incapacitation from further law-violative behavior, or may include deterrence, retribution, or rehabilitation. Commitment results from the decision that some combination of such goals necessitates the deprivation of the inmate's freedom. But it is nowhere spelled out in law or policy that loss of freedom is to be accompanied by random exposure to staff or inmate brutality and sexual or other primitive aggression. Absolutely essential to interpersonal maturity and to socialization is the sense of simple physical security. Assurance of such security might well be considered the first responsibility of the institution. Failure to accomplish it may be expected to result in failure in almost all other positive institutional goals.

2. *Authority structure,* including exposure of the young person to a structure that cannot be evaded, that engenders respect for its strength, but that is dedicatedly, continuously, and very evidently fair, consistent, and imbued with respect for the human dignity of those subject to it. In their homes and in their communities, most juvenile offenders have known long histories of struggle against authority structures that have been vacillating, capricious, unfair, and often cruel. Every aspect of the institution's program must take cognizance of the need to provide a corrective experience in this important area of life.

3. *Role models,* emerging from a close relationship with adults who are themselves committed to a law-abiding way of life, who are deeply concerned about the welfare of their charges, who reject their delinquent behavior but do not reject them, who understand them and their angers and frustrations, and who remain dedicated to helping them grow and realize their own fullest potential. Again, many delinquents have never had such a relationship, and have never known adult role models who could help them envision what they might one day become.

4. *Education,* beginning with a careful assessment of the individual's capacities and achievements and so designed as to help him begin at a point where he can achieve success and move toward mastery of the

academic and vocational skills necessary to functioning as a citizen and as a productive participant in the economic order. Many delinquents have known only lives of frustration and failure. They have had to turn to illegal conquests in order to gain any sense of self-worth. They desperately need to be placed in a situation in which they *can* succeed in a positive way.

5. *Insight*, where help in understanding and mastering the complex peer relationship problems so common to adolescence is offered. This would also entail sensitive individual and group counseling directed at helping the adolescent perceive and digest his daily life experience, develop effective interpersonal skills, make use of the positive experiences available to him, assess his own role in the various situations in which he is involved, and move toward the best possible utilization of his opportunities and capacities.

6. *Reintegration*, based on a continuing process of movement toward establishing meaningful ties with the community from which the delinquent has been temporarily excluded. The ward must be helped to see this as beginning at his admission to the institution and continuing after his release to the free community. Counseling should include a continuing sort of mental rehearsal, preparing for the important elements of and the inevitable problems of the community life to come. Release must be accompanied by careful help in reestablishing positively functioning relationships with family, school or work, and community.

Quite obviously, we are speaking here of the necessity in the correctional institution, as in all other aspects of the transaction between the delinquent and the broader society, for relationships based on honesty, on fundamental respect for human dignity, on understanding, and on reaching for the elements of the positive that reside in all of us—in short, for relationships embodying human decency. In the final analysis, the ultimate test of every rule or regulation, every policy, every transaction must be, "Is it decent?"

Where Do We Go from Here?

Despite the frustrations we have encountered in our efforts to implement services for juvenile offenders, there is no reason to believe that we are destined to perpetuate a series of ill-conceived, poorly designed programs. There are too many well-run programs for us to believe that they cannot exist. Our task is to ensure that we do not become excessively discouraged by the problems of the past. We must learn from and move ahead from the errors of history. It is also fair to remind ourselves that the business we are engaged in—implementing sound programs for juvenile offenders—is, if no longer in its infancy, at best in the midst of toddlerhood. The span between the mid-1960s, when the rhetoric about the failures of juvenile justice began in earnest, and the present may seem painfully lengthy for those who have lived it, enduring the many false starts and the all too few success stories. But if we take a step back and reflect on it all, we should realize that this period is a mere blink in time when one traces the evolution of juvenile misbehavior and the treatment of it. We have accomplished a great deal, in fact, and if much of what we have learned is what *not* to do and is the result of our mistakes, so be it. The bottom line is that the thoughtful and attentive among us *have* learned, and we dare say that this knowlege stands to increase the likelihood that the ratio of successes to failures will become more favorable as time moves on. The greatest tragedy would be the result not of our accumulated failures but of our inability to translate what we have learned into more skillfully and conscientiously designed programs.

Such encomia are only useful if they help us to specify in detail what needs to be done in the future. For one thing, it is patently clear that we need to shore up the quality of the theoretical rationales we use to justify our programs. In too many instances, we have let the proverbial tail wag the dog, as some new theory is introduced to add credibility to an existing set of services. We have been glib in our use of the term "theory," and too often we have not had a clear grasp of why we have done what we have done. Our application of concepts such as "labeling" and "differential association theory" has tended to be simplistic, resulting often in the delivery of services whose tie to a truly theoretical justification is tenuous at best. As LaMar Empey stated in a prophetic essay penned in the early days of the diversion and deinstitutionalization movement, without adequate theory, we develop a strategy of activity rather than systematic strategies (Klein 1979:158). We have found that it does not pay to think inductively in this business.

Having said this, it is important to acknowledge our skepticism about the likelihood that we will be able to construct a grand theory to serve as the monolithic foundation for our programmatic efforts. On the contrary, the theories related to juvenile misbehavior and its treatment seem to grow unabated, with little prospect of locating a common denominator that can tie them together in other than a trivial way. Despite this diversity, we need to justify our strategies of intervention on the basis of more than professional instincts or fancy. A theoretical point of view is necessary if we hope to generalize results from one setting to another and from one population to another. Our convictions about what works and our efforts to promulgate our beliefs need to be grounded in concepts, not anecdotes.

Among the central tasks ahead of us is the refinement of procedures and criteria for sorting out which youths should be committed to secure correctional facilities, which to residential community-based programs (some of which will be secure), and which to programs that provide nonresidential services. There is so much independently gathered yet consistent evidence that annually thousands of youths are referred inappropriately to a variety of corrections programs, resulting in the exacerbation of stigma, strains on staff, excessive or inadequate social control, and increased costs. The lack of rigorous intake and referral procedures is without question one of the weakest links in the juvenile justice chain. Considerable effort needs to be devoted to sound and reliable criteria to determine who goes where and why. When a first-time runaway is relabeled in order to render him eligible for secure detention, or when a violent offender is referred to an underenrolled but poorly run group home in order to help keep the daily census at an acceptable level, everyone loses. Communities that have managed to avoid the problems of net-widening and unanticipated costs tend to be communities that have managed to construct detailed, respected, and enforced intake and referral criteria.

The problems that face that special group of youths who are committed to traditional training schools are well known and documented. The problems with understaffing, inadequate training, funding, facilities, abuse, and morale are legendary by now. Though some institutions have been able to escape these baneful conditions, most have not. The problems persist, even though we tend to know what they are. The lack of community support that stands behind these programs—both monetary and ideological—does not bode well for their future, especially given the waning level of tolerance for juvenile mischief.

The circumstances are somewhat different for noninstitutional programs, in that we seem to be much less certain that we understand what the problems are. As our discussion indicates, however, we are beginning to develop some pretty good hints. We need to pay particular attention to the ways in which we operationalize the concept "community-based" so that the services we provide and the programs we design do approximate the ideal that this term implies. We know that a program is not community-based simply by virtue of its location in a noninstitutional setting. We must more closely examine the prevailing atmospheres in the programs, the surveillance of the youths, the frequency and quality of contact with family, friends, schools, and other community agencies, the rules and disciplinary measures, and the level of support and tolerance from the surrounding community. Many a program that has looked impressive on paper has failed because of the lack of ties with community residents and agencies.

The issue of community tolerance is particularly important. Most communities are at best ambivalent about a program that brings juvenile offenders to reside in them. And their fears are understandable, despite the fact that instances where a neighbor is harmed by a juvenile are relatively rare. If care is not taken to cultivate support, or at least tolerance, the considerable effort devoted to securing funding, recruiting and training staff, locating a facility, and designing services may be for naught.

Two further issues call for much more attention than they have received. The first concerns the trend toward the purchase of services from private vendors. This phenomenon is especially relevant considering the current popularity of the belief that the private sector should be relied on to the greatest extent possible for the resolution of public problems. We must be diligent in our review of the merits and demerits of the intimate relationship that has emerged in recent years between public correctional agencies and private service providers. It would be unfortunate if the contemporary enthusiasm about the ability of free enterprise to address public troubles were to blind us to the real limitations of entrepreneurial corrections, whatever its virtues may be.

In addition, we will need to look beyond the design of programs only for the stereotypical population: street-wise males from metropolitan areas. Insufficient attention has been paid to less visible but compelling groups of juvenile offenders, including females, youths from nonmetropolitan or rural areas, and severely disturbed youths. There is growing evidence that rural youths and females are involved in delinquent and status offenses to a much greater extent than official records tend to indicate. Unfortunately, the vast majority of corrections programs have not been designed with the needs of these particular juveniles in mind. Similarly, remarkably little attention has been paid to the needs of severely disturbed juvenile offenders, who frequently get caught between the boundaries of state correctional and mental health agencies. In many instances, youths who are both dangerous and quite disturbed are relegated to locked wards in an adolescent unit of a state hospital or in a segregation unit of a state training school because of a lack of programs designed specifically for them. Only a handful of states have managed to implement services that attend simultaneously to the security risk these youths pose and to their compelling mental health needs (Reamer and Bederow, 1983–84).

Clearly there is an intimidatingly wide range of issues that demand our attention as we attempt to devise strategies for handling mischievous youths, especially in light of the current emphasis on noninstitutional programs. We must be mindful of the need for clear intake and referral criteria, the risks associated with net-widening and relabeling, due process concerns, the purchase of services from the private sector, the use of coercion in the delivery of services, the community-based character of noninstitutional programs, and the theoretical rationales we use to justify our various ministrations to youthful offenders. Though this list is imposing, we will only perpetuate the problems of juvenile justice if we shy away from it.

CHAPTER 7
FINAL OBSERVATIONS: THE PURSUIT OF JUVENILE JUSTICE

There are few topics in life that are discussed with as much passion as that of crime. Though taxes and death may command as much attention, there at least is widespread acceptance of their inevitability. Not so with crime. Though it has been omnipresent on our landscape throughout history, we seem remarkably unwilling to accept that some level of criminal activity is here to stay. Despite mountains of evidence to the contrary, we persist in our fantasies that criminal activity can be substantially eliminated. In the minds of the public, all we need is the proper armamentaria; with sufficiently staffed police departments and district attorneys' offices, a stern and intolerant judiciary, and certain, severe, well-publicized penalties, our world's miscreants would certainly desist.

Thoughtful veterans of the criminal justice system know better, of course. The problems of crime and delinquency extend far beyond the adequacy of supplies and personnel. Short of converting our neighborhoods into armed camps, we know by now that mere increases in the quality and quantity of law enforcement would do relatively little to affect the criminality that surrounds us. The overwhelming majority of criminal acts are effectively concealed from law enforcement personnel and from common citizens. They probably always will be, no matter how much we enhance our ability to carry out surveillance, prosecution, and incarceration. Those who happen to fall within the grasp of the criminal justice system will no doubt always constitute a small portion of those who violate laws. Claims to the contrary by politicians who campaign on "get tough" platforms or by understandably frustrated citizens are regrettably naive. A more efficient criminal justice system can certainly have a substantial impact on those relatively few lives it touches, but the crux of the problem is much larger in scope and far more complex.

Nevertheless, we are aware that rhetoric about the causal connections between crime and problem-laden families, drugs, crippled school systems, stagnant economies, and so forth, seems hackneyed to those concerned about juvenile delinquency. The litany of problems seems all too familiar, especially given that our multi-billion-dollar, multi-year efforts to shorten the list have not seemed to most observers to be especially effective. The rhetoric seems trite now not because it is void of substance but because in fact we understand the multiple causes of juvenile delinquency rather well. Thus we cannot resist pointing out what have turned out to be terribly intractable problems. There is no question that ill-trained police, lenient judges, and poorly run correctional programs account for a portion of distressingly high recidivism rates. Some youths certainly need more than a slap on the wrist, and our failure to provide it may explain a small percentage of those cases of youths who smirk at the law. Without question, however, the lion's share of juvenile misbehavior can be traced back to social, psychological, and economic factors that dramatically overshadow the influence of the criminal justice system itself.

Cynics who question the claims of social scientists, social workers, and other professionals about the causes of juvenile crime frequently point to the supposed ineffectiveness of years of effort as evidence that our hypotheses are invalid and that "liberal" views about the ways in which juvenile crime ought to be handled are misguided. This assumption is flawed. For one thing, evidence concerning the lack of decline in recidivism rates does not necessarily mean that our assumptions about the root causes of the problem are inaccurate. It is not at all unusual for substantial gaps to exist between our understanding of a problem and our ability to affect it. Consider, for example, contemporary understanding of factors that lead to high rates of unemployment. It is well known that a large federal deficit can inflate interest rates, owing to the government's competition in the market for funds to finance the debt. High interest rates, in turn, discourage borrowing, investment, and construction, which then exacerbates unemployment. Because the government's policy has not substantially reduced unemployment, however, does not mean that it fails to understand its principal causes. Rather, it means that while solutions may be reasonably well understood, the costs involved (for example, in the form of higher inflation rates) may be considered too steep. The same holds for our efforts to deal with crime and delinquency; while there is a great deal we do know about their determinants, the cost of the remedy is thought by many to be too steep, in terms of either dollars and cents, the loss of civil liberties, or the increaased presence of government in the lives of private citizens.

But the major flaw may be that we have simply failed to demonstrate convincingly how much we have in fact accomplished in our attempts to stem crime and delinquency, dwelling instead on our false starts and failures. As we indicated in our discussion of the results of empirical research on program effectiveness, the field's measurement tools and designs are frequently primitive in nature and fail to reveal what effects various interventions have had. Our research inquiries often lack adequate control over the various extraneous factors that can affect youths beyond the rehabilitation and prevention programs themselves. Most of our instrumentation can measure in only a crude way important changes in attitude, behavior, and life circumstances. But, though it is unfortunate that we are not able to document more precisely the effects of our effort with offenders, we should not assume that our programs are ornaments—attractive but functionally useless. This would be akin to assuming that spiritual phenomena do not exist because of our inability to measure them.

We must also be careful not to be swept away by popular assumptions that despite our programs rates of crime and delinquency continue unabated, and therefore that stern measures are called for in response rather than continued commitment to the rehabilitative ideal. One of the distressing things about widespread public opinion on sensitive matters is that it is often impressionable and misinformed. Such, it appears, is the case at present. In 1982, for example, the Opinion Research Corporation of America conducted a national survey of public opinion concerning attitudes toward juvenile crime. According to the results, more than 80 percent of the public believes that the United States is in the midst of a serious juvenile crime wave. Much to the contrary, however, are the Uniform Crime Report data issued by the U.S. Department of Justice and the results of the victimization studies described earlier. The rates for serious property offense and violent crimes committed by juveniles have been rather stable in recent years, with some decline in the 1980s (Schwartz 1984). Thus, efforts to battle the juvenile crime problem may be more effective than the general public knows, though certainly a myriad of other socioeconomic and demographic factors also help to explain these encouraging trends.

Soft Determinism in Juvenile Justice

At this point in our efforts to wrestle with the future, we should concede that the sort of empirical foundation on which we would like to base our programs and interventions does not exist. We have only rough measures of the extent of the problem and of the effectiveness of efforts to deal with it. We should admit this candidly and pursue our attempts to refine our measurement tools, but most of all we should get on with the business of thinking carefully about what can and should be done with juvenile offenders on the basis of the best available knowledge. Let us also admit that no matter how precise and sophisticated our empirical data, public policy with respect to juvenile offenders will continue to be shaped by deep-seated feelings we have about youths who misbehave, as well as by political and personal ideology.

All of us make assumptions about the culpability of juveniles and about the extent to which they ought to be held accountable for their deeds. In our view, the current confusion about the handling of juvenile offenders stems largely from a widespread challenge to the principle of diminished responsibility that has guided the administration of juvenile justice in the United States since the nineteenth century. Scores of us—both professional and lay—have begun to have second (and third) thoughts about the validity of the long-standing claim that juvenile offenders know not what they do, that they are unwitting participants in wayward events. Though we know quite well that some delinquents are true victims of miasmic circumstances into which they have been born, many among us are nonetheless inclined to believe that only so much of their behavior can be explained away or pardoned. In the end we are tempted to believe that much of the responsibility for modern-day youths' misbehavior is indeed theirs; the street-wise fifteen-year-old of the late twentieth century is not at all like the misguided youths who won the hearts of the nineteenth-century child savers.

But how confident are we that the principle of diminished responsibility is antiquated? Not very, apparently, for despite the persistent calls for stricter and more certain punishment of juvenile offenders, there clearly remains a part of us that refuses to give in, that is willing to hold out because of a belief that we will one day come to a satisfactory understanding of the reasons why juveniles misbehave, that these reasons do exist and merely await our discovery. This ambivalence is the hallmark of the current era of juvenile justice.

It is interesting to note that the enduring clash between these positivist and classical schools of thought has until recently been tied primarily to debate about the handling of adult offenders. Whether adult criminals have the capacity to make voluntary choices has always seemed a reasonable question to ask, and the controversy has been full and rich. But historically this line of inquiry has seemed less relevant to juveniles. There have been periods during which youths have been held accountable for their misdeeds, based on an assumption that they freely choose to commit them. But this position has not held sway since the inauguration of the formal juvenile justice system in the nineteenth century. Rather, there has been a noteworthy predisposition to invoke the principle of determinism when dealing with juveniles. In recent years, however, we have begun to hear the language of free will introduced in discussions about juvenile crime with greater and greater frequency. We seem to have begun to ask whether the determinism which we have embraced for so long has begun to show its age. The concepts of prevention, treatment, and rehabilitation have lost favor, while those of punishment, culpability, retribution, and *mens rea* are in ascendancy.

The extent of the ambivalence is reflected in both the diversity of theoretical constructs that are invoked to justify our response to delinquency and in the content of the responses themselves. Among juvenile justice professionals who couch their views in theoretical terms—and many do not—there is what can best be described as a theoretical free-for-all. We have reached a point in the field where no one theoretical view is predominant, where there are roughly as many advocates of positivist points of view as those that stress free will. The range of opinion within the positivist camp itself is impressive, with views that emphasize biological, psychological, economic, demographic, environmental, and familial determinants, among others. Thus, it is no surprise that programs for juvenile offenders range from relaxed counseling services characterized by heavy doses of empathy and support, to strict incarceration in settings where retribution is both expected and encouraged.

Most contemporary programs reflect what can be described as "soft determinism," a term first suggested in a far-sighted work by David Matza (1964). In brief, there must be simultaneous acknowledgment of the determinants of youths' misbehavior and the need for them to accept some measure of responsibility for it. In fact, this view of soft determinism is perhaps the only conceptual tie that links the majority of approaches in juvenile justice today. And for good reason. If we have learned anything as a result of the nearly century-old collection of serious research related to juvenile justice, it is that frequently, though not always, there are compelling reasons why juveniles misbehave. Evidence of the influence of child abuse, emotional and material neglect, alcoholism, drug abuse, poor education and parenting, and the rest of the familiar list is incontrovertible. There is no denying that these various forms of assault matter to children and to their futures, and that an unfortunate by-product sometimes is a youth who does not conform to our day-to-day conventions of behavior. Yet there is also no denying that we are inclined nonetheless to hold youths accountable for some of their misdeeds, communicate our distress to them, and expect them to accept some responsibility for their future, if not for their pasts.

The positions we have expressed in this book reflect this view. There are times when youths must be restrained, admonished, and scolded. They need to be held accountable for harm they inflict on others and expected to live with the consequences of misbehaving. Yet the vast majority of youths who are troublesome know they are in some trouble and will respond to meaningful, sincere attempts to offer aid and support. Offers of ministration will not always be appreciated and will even be scorned at times. Nonetheless, seasoned professionals in the juvenile justice field know in their bones that carefully designed and delivered help can make a difference.

Offerings of Help

Unfortunately, juvenile justice professionals also know that the kind of talent that is necessary to reach offenders and make a difference in their lives and conduct is rare. Programs for this population are frequently staffed by persons who, if they were not hardened and cynical upon their induction into the profession, quickly become so. The scenario frequently unfolds thusly: relatively young, eager faces, fresh with idealism, are attracted to correctional programs because of a sincere belief that what misguided youths need is a fair shake in life and decent, respectful, and empathic care. With refreshing enthusiasm that the naiveté of inexperience fosters, these young professionals charge into a system rife with stagnation, punitiveness, indifference, cynicism, inconsistency, and disingenuousness. True commitment to the values that drive nascent professionals is hard to locate, they discover, and where it can be found it is often camouflaged by pernicious views and policies. Those who do not flee the field quickly become "realists," whose agendas are quickly revised in light of the resistance they face. Though they may not abandon their commitment entirely, their zeal is diluted. There are those, of course, who manage to sustain their devotion to the rehabilitative ideal despite the obstacles on the way, but their numbers are small when placed in the context of the formal juvenile justice system (police, courts, correctional programs) that surrounds them.

It is difficult for most lay people, and even for many professionals in the juvenile justice field, to comprehend how it is possible to care—in the true and nontrite sense of this word—for a human being who has seriously injured another, often with malice. How is it possible to feel even an ounce of compassion for a youth who has perhaps mugged an elderly pedestrian, raped a young mother, broken into homes and terrorized their residents, or perpetrated any other of the endless offenses that juveniles manage to commit? This is a difficult question to answer. Those few professionals who have been able to cultivate genuinely caring relationships with juvenile offenders must wrestle with this question in their own hearts. It would be naive, overly simplistic, and moralistic for us to merely assert that professionals have a duty to aid even those who are cruel, vicious, and thoughtless in their ways. Perhaps we do incur such a duty by dint of our status as professionals. But to argue that professionals should care about juvenile offenders because they are supposed to is pointless. If the springs of action come not from the heart, they are probably not worth nourishing.

It is rare that one finds a chronic or serious offender who has not been the victim of protracted, often bone-chilling abuse or neglect. The records of any correctional program in America will reveal that the majority of offenders have been subjected to any of a number of disturbing assaults upon mind or body, most often beginning in the earliest years of life. Certainly an occasional exception can be uncovered. The undeniable truth of the matter, however, is that youths who hurt are themselves deeply hurt, though the scars are not always visible. The volume and severity of physical and emotional abuse and neglect to which most chronic juvenile offenders have been subjected long before they encountered their first police officer are staggering. This by no means excuses their subsequent misconduct and is not an argument for leniency. These are circumstances that should move us, however, if not to compassion then at least to understanding. The defenses these youths have erected around themselves as a consequence are often inpenetrable, at least in the short run.

If one comes to understand the noisome conditions that serve as a context for these youths' behavior, it is easier to reach a point where one can appreciate how much help these youths need, and how counterproductive continued assaults on them will be. This is not to say that any and all forms of control should be abandoned. Quite the contrary, for structure and limits frequently are just what these youths yearn for (though they may be loath to admit it) and require. However, the sanctions imposed on them cannot reflect mere vindictiveness. If they are to serve any useful purpose whatsoever, they must issue from motives that are constructive rather than destructive.

Juvenile justice professionals must first understand that their clients often resent their presence, distrust them, and will be suspicious of offers of assistance. These youths epitomize the "resistant client." It is difficult to reach them without a candid acknowledgment of the possibility that they harbor skepticism and suspicion about offers of aid. Walls of defensiveness can rarely be crumbled without some verbal admission to these youths that because of their experiences they often have good reason to mistrust professionals who claim that they have come to help. It is important to recognize that many youthful offenders have had extensive encounters with professionals who have seemed disinterested, manipulative, hostile, vindictive, deceptive, or worse. True offers of help must be accompanied not only by sensitivity and sincerity but by such realism as well. It is naive for any professional to assume that offenders will quickly sense genuineness and respond to it. Truly helpful relationships with offenders—relationships that explore beyond the superficial details that occupy many "therapeutic" encounters—tend to evolve slowly and deliberately. Institution-wise youths know to be wary and will reveal themselves to professionals only after an extended period during which limits, trustworthiness, and reliability are tested. In those cases where trust and respect are finally earned by both parties, significant change can in fact occur. It does not always occur and when it does it is ordinarily not without incident. False starts and stumbles frequently interrupt. Marked change can occur, however, and when it does it can be awesome for both youth and professional.

Unfortunately, the interpersonal skills that are called for in order to promote genuinely therapeutic relationships are not of the sort that can be imparted in preprogrammed fashion. Though training curricula, skill-building exercises, and countless other techniques may enhance the professional's ability to communicate with an offender, in the end it is the special character, decency, and sensitivity within the individual worker that matter. Training in interpersonal skills and techniques are often vital but, alone, do not suffice. Sophisticated youths are quick to distinguish canned techniques learned in some workshop from genuine skill and commitment.

The Evolution of Child Saving

We began this book with the observation that the recent history of juvenile justice has been characterized by a decline in the spirit of child saving that surrounded the formal creation of the field in the late nineteenth and early twentieth centuries. The perceptible move away from the forgiving views of the child savers is not entirely inappropriate. Today we are far less naive about the nature of juvenile crime and ways of responding to it than we were at the turn of the century. Solicitous care, nurture, and affection are not enough to alter the ways of many contemporary offenders. Sophisticated treatment, trained professionals, adequate facilities, and an emphasis on due process are essential ingredients in any reasoned effort to confront the modern-day variety of juvenile crime. The relative simplicity and paternalism of the child saving days are now obsolete.

Yet, in our pursuit of updated measures to handle today's offenders, we seem to have lost a particular virtue of the child savers. No matter what one believes about the motives of the principals of that movement—whether or not one accepts the cynical assessments of that era—

the optimism and faith in youths that moved the child savers have largely evaporated. Professionals and lay citizens alike can find little good and few rays of hope in many of today's youths. Instead, it is commonly believed that the passage of time has created a species of juvenile distinctly different from yesterday's: one more vicious, callous, and self-righteous. The extent to which this assertion is true is hard to assess or to document. Views on the subject are influenced as much by advances in methods of detecting and recording crime as by actual changes in character and behavior. Nonetheless, what matters is that there is widespread *belief* that for today's youths the velvet glove must give way to the iron fist, and as a result the relationship between the components of the juvenile justice system and youths has evolved into one in which antagonism and distrust fill the air. The ability of the professional to genuinely care about a juvenile in such a climate is sorely tested—and this feature of contemporary juvenile justice more than any other portends a difficult future. Difficult, that is, if we accept the inevitability of the climate that currently envelopes juvenile justice. Such need not be the case, if we are willing to examine critically and nondefensively the means and motives we have erected for dealing with juvenile offenders in our police districts, juvenile and family courts, and correctional programs. There are success stories nationwide that would inspire if only we would dwell on them as much as we do our failures. Unfortunately, it seems fashionable to publicize the casualties of juvenile justice, and to overlook and sometimes bury that which we have done well.

It is myopic for those concerned with juvenile crime to be preoccupied with youths who get caught. This portion of the problem, though significant in its own right, is a mere by-product of the fundamental one: the quality of the society that has somehow managed to produce the youths whom we resent with such passion. It is true that juvenile offenders themselves must be held responsible for their behavior. Fancy etiological theories have their limits, and in the final analysis it is each offender's behavior that we must seek to control. Conceding this, however, we must be careful not to be seduced into blaming the victim in all instances. This is much too convenient and self-deluding. Much of the responsibility is ours and lies in the defect-laden communities, schools, and families into which these youths have been born. If we look beyond our mirrors rather than in them, we are likely to miss the problem.

Human behavior will always be mysterious, especially when it departs from the conventional. Despite decades of formal inquiry into the subject, all of us still have the capacity to be surprised by the twists and turns of people's lives. Those we think we understand sometimes behave in ways we never imagined possible. Sometimes their aberrations make national headlines, as in the numerous cases of esteemed public officials "caught in the act." Sometimes they furnish nothing more than whispered gossip over the backyard fence. Our knowledge is grossly imperfect, and our frequent failures of prediction should serve to keep us humble and remind us that sweeping statements about misbehavior—about both its causes and its cures—are presumptuous. There is no doubt that we have the capacity to alter some behavior in some youths in some instances. This is probably the best we can ever hope to achieve, unless we resort to drastic measures of control that citizens of a democracy—no matter how flawed—would not tolerate. Our principal task is to acknowledge the complexity of the challenge, along with the responsibility both we and youthful offenders share in pursuing it. Most of all we must acknowledge the enigmatic features of human nature that both permit youthful misbehavior and make inevitable the difficulty we have in responding to it.

References

Adams, Stuart. 1976. "Evaluation: A Way Out of Rhetoric." In *Reha-bilitation, Recidivism, and Research,* ed. National Council on Crime and Delinquency. Hackensack, N.J.: The Council.

Aichorn, August. 1935. *Wayward Youth.* New York: Viking Press.

Alexander, Franz G., and Hugo Staub. 1956. *The Criminal, the Judge, and the Public.* Rev. ed. Glencoe, Ill.: Free Press.

Allen, Francis R. 1964. *Borderland of Criminal Justice.* Chicago: University of Chicago Press.

—— 1981. *The Decline of the Rehabilitative Ideal: Penal Policy and Social Purpose.* New Haven and London: Yale University Press.

American Correctional Association. 1981. "Juveniles Commit One Fourth of Violent Personal Crimes." *On the Line* 4(7):11–12.

Andenaes, Johannes. 1974. *Punishment and Deterrence.* Ann Arbor: University of Michigan Press.

Asquith, Stewart. 1983a. *Children and Justice: Decision-Making in Children's Hearings and Juvenile Courts.* Edinburgh: Edinburgh University Press.

—— 1983b. "Justice, Retribution, and Children." In *Providing Criminal Justice for Children,* ed. Allison Morris and Henri Geller, pp. 7–19. London and Baltimore: Edward Arnold.

Austin, James and Barry Krisberg. 1981. "Wider, Stronger, and Different Nets: The Dialectics of Criminal Justice Reform." *Journal of Research in Crime and Delinquency* 18:165–96.

Bailey, Kenneth D. 1982. *Methods of Social Research.* 2d ed. New York: Free Press.

Barkwell, Lawrence J. 1980. "Differential Probation Treatment of Delinquency." In *Effective Correctional Treatment,* ed. Robert R. Ross and Paul Gendreau, pp. 279–98. Toronto: Butterworth.

Bartollas, Clemens, Stuart J. Miller, and Simon Dinitz. 1976. *Juvenile Victimization: The Institutional Paradox.* New York: Wiley.

Baxstrom v. Herold, 383 U.S. 107 (1966).

Becker, Howard S. 1963. *The Outsiders: Studies in the Sociology of Deviance.* New York: Free Press of Glencoe.

Bentham, Jeremy. [1789] 1973. "An Introduction to the Principles of Morals and Legislation." In *The Utilitarians,* pp. 7–398. New York: Anchor Books.

Berman, Sidney. 1959. "Antisocial Character Disorder: Its Etiology and Relationship to Delinquency." *American Journal of Orthopsychiatry* 29:612–21.

Binder, Arnold and Gilbert Geis. 1984. "Ad Populum Argumentation in Criminology: Juvenile Diversion as Rhetoric." *Crime and Delinquency* 30(2):309–33.

Black, Donald J. and Albert J. Reiss, Jr. 1970. "Police Control of Juveniles." *American Sociological Review* (February) 35:63–77.

Bloch, Herbert A. and Arthur Niederhoffer. 1958. *The Gang: A Study in Adolescent Behavior.* New York: Philosophical Library.

Blumstein, Alfred, Jacqueline Cohen, and Daniel Nagin, eds. 1978. *Deterrence and Incapacitation: Estimating the Effects of Criminal Sanctions on Crime Rates.* Report of the Panel on Research and Deterrent and Incapacitative Effects, National Academy of Sciences. Washington, D.C.: The Academy.

Bohnstedt, Marvin. 1978. "Answers to Three Questions About Juvenile Diversion." *Journal of Research in Crime and Delinquency* 15:109–23.

Breed v. Jones, 421 U.S. 519 (1975).

Brodbeck, May. 1968. "Explanation, Prediction, and 'Imperfect Knowledge.'" In *Readings in the Philosophy of the Social Sciences,* ed. May Brodbeck. New York: Macmillan.

California Department of the Youth Authority. n.d. *The Community Treatment Project After Five Years.* Sacramento: The Department.

Chaiken, Jan M. and Marcia R. Chaiken. 1983. "Trends and Targets." *Wilson Quarterly* 7:106.

Cicourel, Aaron. 1968. *The Social Organization of Juvenile Justice.* New York: Wiley.

Cloward, Richard A. and Lloyd E. Ohlin. 1960. *Delinquency and Opportunity.* New York: Free Press.

Coates, Robert B., Alden D. Miller, and Lloyd E. Ohlin. 1978. *Diversity in a Youth Correctional System.* Cambridge, Mass.: Ballinger.

Cohen, Albert K. 1955. *Delinquent Boys: The Culture of the Gang.* Glencoe, Ill.: Free Press.

Cohen, Jacqueline. 1978. "The Incapacitative Effect of Imprisonment: A Critical Review of the Literature." In *Deterrence and Incapacitation: Estimating the Effects of Criminal Sanctions on Crime Rates,* ed. Alfred Blumstein, Jacqueline Cohen, and Daniel Nagin, pp. 187–243. Report of the Panel on Research on Deterrent and Incapacitative Effects, National Research Council, National Academy of Sciences. Washington, D.C.: The Academy.

Cohen, L. E. and J. R. Kluegel. 1978. "Determinants of Juvenile Court Dispositions: Ascriptive and Achieved Factors in Two Metropolitan Courts." *American Sociological Review* 43(2):162–76.

Cohen, Stanley. 1979. "The Punitive City: Notes on the Dispersal of Social Control." *Contemporary Crisis* 3:343.

Commonwealth v. Fisher, Supreme Court of Pennsylvania, 1905. 213 Pa. 48, 62A198.

Conrad, John. 1981. "Can Juvenile Justice Survive?" *Crime and Delinquency* 27:544–54.

Cook, Philip J. 1980. "Research in Criminal Deterrence: Laying the Groundwork for the Second Decade." In *Crime and Justice: An Annual Review of Research,* ed. Norval Morris and Michael Tonry, 2:221–68. Chicago: University of Chicago Press.

Cullen, Francis T. and Karen Gilbert. 1982. *Reaffirming Rehabilitation.* Cincinnati: Anderson.

Doleschal, Eugene and Nora Klapmuts. 1973. "Toward a New Criminology." *Crime and Delinquency Literature* 5(4):607–26.

Dunford, Franklyn W. 1977. "Police Diversion: An Illusion?" *Criminology* 15:338.

Elliott, Delbert. 1980. "Recurring Issues in the Evaluation of Delinquency Prevention and Treatment Programs." In *Critical Issues in Juvenile Delinquency,* ed. David Shichor and Delos H. Kelly, pp. 237–61. Lexington, Mass.: Lexington Books.

Empey, La Mar T. 1978. *American Delinquency: Its Meaning and Construction.* Homewood, Ill.: Dorsey.

Empey, La Mar T. and Maynard L. Erickson. 1972. *The Provo Experiment: Evaluating Community Control of Delinquency.* Lexington, Mass.: D. C. Heath.

Empey, La Mar T. and Steven G. Lubeck. 1971. *The Silverlake Experiment: Testing Delinquency Theory and Community Intervention.* Chicago: Aldine.

Erickson, Maynard L. 1979. "Some Empirical Questions Concerning the Current Revolution in Juvenile Justice." In *The Future of*

Childhood and Juvenile Justice, ed. La Mar T. Empey, pp. 277–311. Charlottesville: University Press of Virginia.

Ezorsky, Gertrude, ed. 1972. *Philosophical Perspectives on Punishment.* Albany: State University of New York Press.

Fagan, Jeffrey, Sally Jo Jones, Eliot Hartstone, Cary Rudman, and Robert Emerson. 1981. *Background Paper for the Violent Juvenile Offender Research and Development Program.* Submitted to Office of Juvenile Justice and Delinquency Prevention, U.S. Department of Justice. San Francisco: URSA Institute.

Fogel, David. 1979. *. . . We Are the Living Proof: The Justice Model for Corrections.* 2d ed. Cincinnati: Anderson.

Foster, Jack Donald. 1972. "Perceptions of Stigma Following Public Intervention for Delinquent Behavior." *Social Problems* (Fall) 20:202–9.

Fox, Sanford J. 1974. "The Reform of Juvenile Justice: The Child's Right to Punishment." *Juvenile Justice* 25:2–9.

Freund, William C. 1982. "The Looming Impact of Population Changes." *Wall Street Journal,* April 6, p. 1.

Friedlander, Kate. 1947. *The Psychoanalytic Approach to Juvenile Delinquency: Theory, Case Studies, and Treatment.* New York: International University Press.

Galvin, Jim and Kenneth Polk. 1982. "Any Truth You Want: The Use and Abuse of Crime and Criminal Justice Statistics." *Journal of Research in Crime and Delinquency* 19(1):135–65.

Garnett, W. H. Stuart. 1911. *Children and the Law.* London: John Murray.

Garofalo, James. 1979. "Victimization and Fear of Crime." *Journal of Research in Crime and Delinquency* 16(1):80–97.

Gaylin, Willard and David Rothman. 1976. "Introduction." In Andrew von Hirsch, *Doing Justice: The Choice of Punishments,* pp. 21–41. New York: Hill and Wang.

Glaser, Daniel. 1979. "A Review of Crime-Causation Theory and Its Application." In *Crime and Justice: An Annual Review of Research,* ed. Norval Morris and Michael Tonry. Vol. 1. Chicago: University of Chicago Press.

Greenberg, David F. 1977. "The Correctional Effects of Corrections: A Survey of Evaluations." In *Corrections and Punishment,* ed. David F. Greenberg, pp. 111–48. Beverly Hills: Sage.

Gurr, Ted Robert. 1980. "On the History of Violent Crime in Europe and America." In *Criminology Review Year Book,* ed. Egon Bittner and Sheldon Messinger, 2:411–32. Beverly Hills and London: Sage.

—— 1981. "Historical Trends in Violent Crimes: A Critical Review of the Evidence." In *Crime and Justice: An Annual Review of Research,* ed. Michael Tonry and Norval Morris, 3:295–353. Chicago: University of Chicago Press.

Haapanen, Rudy A. and Carl F. Jesness. 1982. *Early Identification of the Chronic Offender: Executive Summary.* Sacramento: Department of the Youth Authority (February).

Hamparian, Donna Martin, Richard Schuster, Simon Dinitz, and John P. Conrad. 1978. *The Violent Few: A Study of Dangerous Juvenile Offenders.* Lexington, Mass.: Lexington Books, D.C. Heath.

Hasenfeld, Yeheskel. 1976. "Youth in Juvenile Court: Input and Output Patterns." In *Brought to Justice? Juveniles, the Courts, and the Law,* ed. Rosemary Sarri and Yeheskel Hasenfeld. Ann Arbor: National Assessment of Juvenile Corrections, University of Michigan.

Haugen, Daniel, Theresa Costello, Ira Schwartz, Barry Krisberg, and Paul Litsky. n.d. [April 1982] *Summary of National Public Opinion Survey, Public Attitudes Toward Youth Crime.* Minneapolis: Hubert H. Humphrey Institute of Public Affairs and School of Social Work, University of Minnesota and the Field Institute. Summary privately distributed.

Hazard, Geoffrey C. 1976. "The Jurisprudence of Juvenile Deviance." In *Pursuing Justice for the Child,* ed. Margaret K. Rosenheim, pp. 3–19. Chicago: University of Chicago Press.

Healy, William and Augusta Bronner. 1936. *New Light on Delinquency and Its Treatment.* New Haven: Yale University Press.

Hellum, Frank R. and John Peterson. 1983. "Offense Patterns of Status Offenders." In *Community Treatment of Juvenile Offenders: The DSO Experiments,* ed. Solomon Kobrin and Malcolm W. Klein. Beverly Hills: Sage.

Hindelang, Michael J., Michael R. Gottfredson, and Timothy J. Flanagan. 1981. *Sourcebook of Criminal Justice Statistics—1980.* U.S. Department of Justice, Bureau of Justice Statistics. Washington, D.C.: Government Printing Office.

Hirschi, Travis, 1969. *Causes of Delinquency.* Berkeley: University of California Press.

—— 1980. "Labelling Theory and Juvenile Delinquency: An Assessment of the Evidence." In *The Labeling of Deviance: Evaluating a Perspective,* ed. Walter R. Gove. 2d ed. Beverly Hills and London: Sage.

Howell, James C. and Barbara Allen-Hagen. 1982. "A Closer Look at Juvenile Justice Standards." *Corrections Today* 44(3):28–29, 32–34.

Hurley, Timothy D. 1907. *Origin of the Illinois Juvenile Court Law.* Chicago: Visitation and Aid Society.

Hylton, John H. 1982. "Rhetoric and Reality: A Critical Appraisal of Community Correctional Programs." *Crime and Delinquency* 28:341–73.

In Re Gault. Supreme Court of the United States, 1967. 387 U.S. 1, 87 S. Ct. 1428, 18 L. Ed., 2d. 527.

In Re Winship. Supreme Court of the United States, 1970. 397 U.S. 358, 90 S. Ct. 1068, 25 L. Ed. 2d. 368.

Ingel, Dwight. 1976. *Is It Really So?* Philadelphia: Westminster Press.

Institute of Judicial Administration–American Bar Association Juvenile Justice Standards Project. 1977. *Standards Relating to Transfer Between Courts.* Cambridge, Mass.: Ballinger.

Jenkins, Richard L. and Lester Hewitt. 1944. "Types of Personality Structure Encountered in Child Guidance Clinics." *American Journal of Orthopsychiatry* 14(1):84–94.

Jesness, Carl F. 1965. *The Fricot Ranch Study.* Sacramento: California Youth Authority.

—— 1975. "Comparative Effectiveness of Behavior Modification and Transactional Programs for Delinquents." *Journal of Consulting and Clinical Psychology* 43(6):758–99.

Kahn, Alfred J. 1953. *A Court for Children.* New York: Columbia University Press.

Kent v. United States. Supreme Court of the United States, 1966. 383 U.S. 541, 86 S. Ct. 1045, 16 L. Ed. 2d. 84.

Klein, Malcolm W. 1979. "Deinstitutionalization and Diversion of Juvenile Offenders: A Litany of Impediments." In *Crime and Justice: An Annual Review of Research,* ed. Norval Morris and Michael Tonry, 1:158. Chicago: University of Chicago Press.

Kobrin, Solomon and Malcolm W. Klein. 1983. *Community Treatment of Juvenile Offenders: The DSO Experiments.* Beverly Hills: Sage.

Kozol, H., R. Boucher, and R. Garofolo. 1972. "The Diagnosis and Treatment of Dangerousness." *Crime and Delinquency* 8:371–92.

Krisberg, Barry and Ira Schwartz. 1983. "Rethinking Juvenile Justice." *Crime and Delinquency* 29(3):333–64.

Kuhn, Thomas. 1970. *The Structure of Scientific Revolutions.* 2d ed. Chicago: University of Chicago Press.

Lemert, Edwin M. 1967. "The Juvenile Court—Quest and Realities." In *Task Force Report: Juvenile Delinquency and Youth Crime,* President's Commission on Law Enforcement and Administration of Justice. Washington, D.C.: Government Printing Office.

Lerman, Paul. 1975. *Community Treatment and Social Control.* Chicago: University of Chicago Press.

—— 1980. "Trends and Issues in the Deinstitutionalization of Youths in Trouble." *Crime and Delinquency* 26:281–98.

Liazos, Alexander. 1979. "Capitalism, Socialism, and Delinquency." In *The Future of Childhood and Juvenile Justice,* ed. La Mar T. Empey. Charlottesville: University Press of Virginia.

Linn, Janice, Kim Zalent, William A. Geller, and Harris Meyer. 1979. *Minors in Need: A Study of Status Offenders at the Juvenile Court of Cook County.* Chicago: Chicago Law Enforcement Study Group.

Lipton, D., R. Martinson, and J. Weeks. 1975. *The Effectiveness of Correctional Treatment.* New York: Praeger.

Livermore, J., C. Malmquist, and P. Meehl. 1968. "On the Justification for Civil Commitment." *University of Pennsylvania Law Review* 117:75–96.

McCord, Joan. 1978. "A Thirty Year Follow-up of Treatment Effects." *American Psychologist* 33(3):284–89. Reprinted in *Criminology Review Year Book,* ed. Sheldon Messinger and Egon Bittner, 1:688–93. Beverly Hills: Sage, 1979.

MacIntyre, Alasdair. 1981. *After Virtue.* Notre Dame, Ind.: University of Notre Dame Press.

Mack, Julian W. 1909. "The Juvenile Court." *Harvard Law Review* 23:104–22.

McKeiver v. Pennsylvania, 403 U.S. 528 (1971).

Mahoney, A. R. 1974. "The Effects of Labeling upon Youths in the Juvenile Justice System." *Law and Society Review* 8:583–614.

Martinson, Robert. 1974. "What Works? Questions and Answers About Prison Reform." *The Public Interest* 35:22–54.

—— 1976. "Evaluation in Crisis—A Postscript." In *Rehabilitation, Recidivism, and Research,* ed. National Council on Crime and Delinquency. Hackensack, N.J.: The Council.

—— 1979. "New Findings, New Views: A Note of Caution Regarding Sentencing Reform." *Hofstra Law Review* 7(2):243–58.

Matza, David. 1964. *Delinquency and Drift.* New York: Wiley.

Mednick, Sarnoff A. and Jan Volavka. 1980. "Biology and Crime." In *Crime and Justice: An Annual Review of Research,* ed. Norval Morris and Michael Tonry, 2:321–80 Chicago: University of Chicago Press.

Mill, John Stuart. [1849] 1943. "On Liberty." In *The Utilitarians,* pp. 474–600. New York: Anchor Books.

Monahan, John. 1978. "The Prediction of Violent Criminal Behavior: A Methodological Critique and Prospectus." In *Deterrence and Incapacitation: Estimating the Effects of Criminal Sanctions on Crime Rates,* ed. Alfred Blumstein, Jacqueline Cohen, and Daniel Nagin, pp. 244–269. Report of the Panel on Research on Deterrent and Incapacitative Effects, National Research Council, National Academy of Sciences. Washington, D.C.: The Academy.

—— 1981. *Predicting Violent Behavior.* Beverly Hills: Sage.

Morris, Norval. 1974. *The Future of Imprisonment.* Chicago: University of Chicago Press.

Murray, Charles A. and Louis A. Cox, Jr. 1979. *Beyond Probation: Juvenile Corrections and the Chronic Delinquent.* Beverly Hills: Sage.

Nagin, Daniel. 1978. "General Deterrence: A Review of the Empirical Evidence." In *Deterrence and Incapacitation: Estimating the Effects of Criminal Sanctions on Crime Rates,* ed. Alfred Blumstein, Jacqueline Cohen, and Daniel Nagin. Report of the Panel on Research on Deterrent and Incapacitative Effects, National Academy of Sciences. Washington, D.C.: The Academy.

National Council on Crime and Delinquency. 1984. *Rethinking Juvenile Justice: Implications for Illinois, Statistical Trends.* Monograph prepared for a conference in Illinois, September 14, 1984. Pages unnumbered. San Francisco: The Council.

Nejelski, Paul. 1976. "Diversion: Unleashing the Hound of Heaven." In *Pursuing Justice for the Child,* ed. Margaret K. Rosenheim, pp. 94–118. Chicago: University of Chicago Press.

Palmer, Ted. 1973. *The Community Treatment Project in Perspective.* Community Treatment Project Series, no. 1. Sacramento: Department of the Youth Authority.

—— 1974. "The Youth Authority's Community Treatment Project." *Federal Probation* 38(1):3–14.

—— 1975. "Martinson Revisited." *Journal of Research in Crime and Delinquency* 12:133–52.

—— 1976. "Abstract: Martinson Revisited." *Crime and Delinquency* 22(2):178–9.

Parsons, Talcott. 1949. *The Structure of Social Action.* Glencoe, Ill.: Free Press.

Pease, Ken and William McWilliams. 1980. *Community Service by Order.* Edinburgh: Scottish Academic Press.

Petersilia, Joan. 1980. "Criminal Career Research: A Review of Recent Evidence." In *Crime and Justice: An Annual Review of Research,* ed. Michael Tonry and Norval Morris, 2:321–78. Chicago: University of Chicago Press.

Piliavin, Irving and Scott Briar. 1964. "Police Encounters with Juveniles." *American Journal of Sociology* (September) 70:206–14.

Platt, Anthony M. 1977. *The Child Savers: The Invention of Delinquency.* 2d ed. Chicago: University of Chicago Press.

Pontell, Henry N. 1978. "Deterrence Theory Versus Practice." *Criminology* 16(1):3–22.

Popper, Karl. 1950. "Indeterminism in Quantum Physics and in Classical Physics, Part 1." *British Journal for the Philosophy of Science* 1:117–33.

Powers, E. and H. Witmer. 1951. *An Experiment in the Prevention of Delinquency: The Cambridge-Somerville Youth Study.* New York: Columbia University Press.

President's Commission on Law Enforcement and the Administration of Justice. 1967. *Task Force Report: Juvenile Delinquency and Youth Crime.* Washington, D.C.: Government Printing Office.

Quinney, Richard. 1970. *The Problem of Crime.* New York: Dodd, Mead.

Reamer, Frederic G. 1982. *Ethical Dilemmas in Social Service.* New York: Columbia University Press.

Reamer, Frederic G. and Laurie S. Bederow. 1983–84. "Caring for Severely Disturbed Juvenile Offenders: Problems and Prospects." *Juvenile and Family Court Journal* 34:59–69.

Reamer, Frederic G., and Charles H. Shireman. 1981. "Alternatives to the Juvenile Justice System: Their Development and the Current State-of-the-Art." *Juvenile and Family Court Journal* 32:17–32.

Redl, Fritz and David Wineman. 1951. *Children Who Hate.* Glencoe, Ill.: Free Press.

Reid, Sue Titus. 1976. *Crime and Criminology.* Hinsdale, Ill.: Dryden Press.

Research and Forecasts, Inc., with Ardy Friedberg. 1983. *The Figgie Report on the Fear of Crime: America Afraid.* New York: New American Library.

Robison, James and Gerald Smith. 1971. "The Effectiveness of Correctional Programs." *Crime and Delinquency* (January) 17:67–80.

Romig, Dennis A. 1978. *Justice for Children.* Lexington, Mass.: D. C. Heath.

Rosenheim, Margaret K., ed. 1962. *Justice for the Child: The Juvenile Court in Transition.* New York: Free Press of Glencoe.

Ross, Robert R. and Paul Gendreau. 1980. *Effective Correctional Treatment*. Toronto: Butterworth.

Rubin, H. Ted. 1979. *Juvenile Justice Policy, Practice, and Law*. Santa Monica: Goodyear.

Rutter, Michael and Henri Giller. 1984. *Juvenile Delinquency: Trends and Perspectives*. New York and London: Guilford Press.

Sanders, Wiley B., ed. 1970. *Juvenile Offenders for a Thousand Years: Selected Readings from Anglo-Saxon Times to 1900*. Chapel Hill: University of North Carolina Press.

Schneider, Peter R., William Griffith, and Anne L. Schneider. 1982. "Juvenile Restitution as a Sole Sanction or Condition of Probation: An Empirical Analysis." *Journal of Research in Crime and Delinquency* (January) 19:47–65.

Schultz, J. Lawrence. 1983. "The Cycle of Juvenile Court History." *Crime and Delinquency* 19(4):457–76.

Schur, Edwin M. 1973. *Radical Nonintervention: Rethinking the Delinquency Problem*. Englewood Cliffs, N.J.: Prentice-Hall.

Schwartz, Ira. 1984. "Getting Tough with Juveniles: Is It Working?" *Public Welfare* (Summer) 42:40–41.

Serril, Michael S. 1980. "Washington's New Juvenile Code." *Corrections Magazine* 6(1):36–41.

Shaw, Clifford R. 1929. *Delinquency Areas*. Chicago: University of Chicago Press.

Shaw, Clifford R. and Henry D. McKay. [1942] 1969. *Juvenile Delinquency and Urban Areas*. Chicago: University of Chicago Press.

Sheldon, William. 1949. *Varieties of Delinquent Youth: An Introduction to Constitutional Psychiatry*. New York: Harper.

Shireman, Charles. 1981. "The Juvenile Justice System: Structure, Problems, and Prospects." In *Justice as Fairness: Perspectives in the Justice Model*, ed. David Fogel and Joe Hudson, pp. 121–59. Cincinnati: Anderson.

Shore, Milton F. and Joseph L. Massimo. 1979. "Fifteen Years After Treatment: A Follow-Up Study of Comprehensive Vocationally-Oriented Psychotherapy." *American Journal of Orthopsychiatry* 49(2):240–45.

Silberman, Charles E. 1978. *Criminal Violence, Criminal Justice*. New York: Random House.

Skogon, Wesley G. and Michael G. Maxfield. 1981. *Coping with Crime: Individual and Neighborhood Reactions*. Beverly Hills: Sage.

Smith, Charles P., Paul S. Alexander, Thomas V. Halatyn, and Chester

T. Roberts. 1979. *A National Assessment of Serious Juvenile Crime and the Juvenile System: The Need for a Rational Response*. Volume 2, *Definition, Characteristics of Incidents and Individuals, and Relationship to Substance Abuse*. Reports of the National Juvenile Justice Assessment Center. Washington, D.C.: Government Printing Office.

Sobie, Merril. 1981. *The Juvenile Offender Act: A Study of the Act's Effectiveness and Impact on the New York Juvenile Justice System*. New York: Foundation for Child Development.

Sparks, Richard F. 1981. "Surveys of Victimization: An Optimistic Assessment." In *Crime and Justice: An Annual Review of Research*, ed. Michael Tonry and Norval Morris. Vol. 3. Chicago: University of Chicago Press.

Spencer, Gregory. 1984. *Projections of the Population of the U.S., by Age, Sex, and Race: 1983 to 2080*. U.S. Bureau of the Census, Current Population Reports, ser. P-25, no. 952. Washington, D.C.: Government Printing Office.

Spergel, Irving A., James P. Lynch, Frederic G. Reamer, and John Korbelik. 1982. "Response of Organization and Community to a Deinstitutionalization Strategy." *Crime and Delinquency* 28:426–49.

Spergel, Irving A., Frederic G. Reamer, and James P. Lynch. 1981. "Deinstitutionalization of Status Offenders: Individual Outcome and System Effects." *Journal of Research in Crime and Delinquency* 18:4–33.

Street, David, Robert D. Vinter, and Charles Perrow. 1966. *Organization for Treatment: A Comparative Study of Institutions for Delinquents*. New York: Free Press.

Sutherland, Edwin. 1972. "Theory of Differential Association." In *Juvenile Delinquency: A Book of Readings*, ed. Rose Giallombardo. 2d ed. New York: Wiley.

Sutherland, Edwin H. and Donald R. Cressey. 1966. *Principles of Criminology*. 7th ed. Philadelphia and New York: J. B. Lippincott.

Tannenbaum, Frank. [1938] 1951. *Crime and the Community*. 2d ed. New York: Columbia University Press.

Terry, Robert. 1967. "Discrimination in the Handling of Juvenile Offenders by Social Control Agencies." *Journal of Research in Crime and Delinquency* (July) 4:218–30.

Thornberry, Terence P. 1973. "Race, Socioeconomic Status and Sentencing in the Juvenile Justice System." *Journal of Criminal Law and Criminology* 64:90–98.

Time Magazine. 1977. "The Youth Crime Plague." July 11, pp. 18–28.

Tuthill, Richard S. 1904. "History of the Children's Court in Chicago." In *Children's Courts in the United States*, ed. Samuel J. Barrows. Washington, D.C.: Government Printing Office.

Twentieth Century Fund, Task Force on Sentencing Policy Toward Youthful Offenders. 1978. *Confronting Youth Crime*. New York: Holmes and Meier.

U.S. Bureau of Census. 1984. *Statistical Abstract of the United States*. Washington, D.C.: Government Printing Office.

U.S. Bureau of Justice Statistics Bulletin. 1984. *Households Touched by Crime, 1983*. Washington, D.C.: National Criminal Justice Reference Service.

U.S. Department of Justice. 1978. *Criminal Victimization in the United States*. Washington, D.C.: Government Printing Office.

U.S. Federal Bureau of Investigation. Yearly. *Uniform Crime Reports: Crime in the United States*. Washington, D.C.: Government Printing Office.

Vinter, Robert D. 1967. "The Juvenile Court as an Institution." In *Task Force Report: Juvenile Delinquency and Youth Crime*, President's Commission on Law Enforcement and Administration of Justice. Washington, D.C.: Government Printing Office.

Wall Street Journal. 1982. "Death on the Road." May 4, p. 1.

Wellford, Charles L. 1973. "Age Composition and the Increase in Recorded Crime." *Criminology* 11:61–70.

Wenk, E., J. Robison, and G. Smith. 1972. "Can Violence Be Predicted?" *Journal of Research in Crime and Delinquency* 18:393–402.

Whitaker, J. Michael and Lawrence J. Severy. 1984. "Service Accountability and Recidivism for Diverted Youth: A Client-and-Service-Comparison Analysis." *Criminal Justice and Behavior* 11(1):35–46.

Wicker, Tom. 1982. "Making Things Worse." *New York Times*. July 9.

Wilson, James Q. 1975. *Thinking about Crime*. New York: Basic Books.

Wolfgang, Marvin E., Robert M. Figlio, and Thorsten Sellin. 1972. *Delinquency in a Birth Cohort*. Chicago: University of Chicago Press.

Zimring, Franklin E. 1981. "Kids, Groups, and Crime: Some Implications of a Well-Known Secret." *Journal of Criminal Law and Criminology* 72(3):867–85.

Zimring, Franklin E. and G. J. Hawkins. 1973. *Deterrence: The Legal Threat in Crime*. Chicago: University of Chicago Press.

Index